Christmas

REINSPECTED

Robert Simms

To
my two
sons, who both
follow Christ with
courage and have always
made me proud of them, and
to my grandchildren, in whom I
see the hope of tomorrow's kingdom
of God.

Christmas

REINSPECTED

*Thoughts on
the Real Christmas Story
—the one in the Bible*

Robert Simms

Except as otherwise marked, scriptures are from the
King James Version of the Bible.

Nativity image on the cover used by permission from:
https://www.freepik.com/vectors/christmas

ISBN: 978-1-7378117-0-1
Published in the United States by
Robert F. Simms
Greer, South Carolina

CONTENTS

1

What Is Christmas? 9

2

The Challenge of Christmas 24

3

Capturing Creation For Christmas 39

4

The Simple Facts of Christmas 50

5

Jesus Was God's Idea 72

6

Are There Any Shepherds Here? 83

7

The Songs of Christmas. 94

8

Jesus' Secret Identity. 103

9

The Innkeeper Who Was Not There 113

10

Pondering Christmas 126

11

The Agony of Christmas 139

12

Why Does Christmas Make Us Afraid? 150

13

Born To Be King 164

14

Dreams of Christmas 174

15

Christmas is Not an Island 193

1

What Is Christmas?
(Luke 2:14)

Bring up the subject of the celebration of Christmas among most Protestants and Catholics in America these days and you won't provoke any real controversy about what Christmas is. Bring up the subject among entirely secular persons and you probably won't get much controversy there, either, but the answer will be very different. The fact is that Christmas, the celebration taking place on and around December 25 of each year, is widely defined depending on who's doing the celebrating.

This book offers no apology for taking a thoroughly biblical view and offering entirely biblical definitions and observations about Christmas. The whole point of this little volume is to reinspect Christmas from what the Bible says.

It should be noted first, as is obvious, that the Bible does not contain the word "Christmas." It doesn't instruct us to celebrate Christmas. We invented it. To be sure, we didn't invent it out of whole cloth: the basis for the celebration is entirely biblical. But God didn't tell Christians to celebrate whatever it is they celebrate at Christmas.

Compared to the Jewish system of sacrifices and feasts, there are precious few things Christians are formally obligated to observe. Catholics have seven sacraments, and three of them aren't required of all Catholics. But among Protestants, there are only two ordinances.

- Jesus told his disciples to observe the Ordinance of Baptism, what Catholics call the Sacrament of Baptism. The command was part of the Great Commission (Mat 28:19).
- He also commanded his followers to remember his sacrifice on the cross by taking the bread and the cup of what Catholics call Holy Communion or the Eucharist and what most Protestants call The Lord's Supper (1 Cor 11:25, et al).
- But even Resurrection Day (what most of the world calls Easter) is not a required Christian celebration. Christians (except Seventh-Day Adventists) already worship on Sunday instead of Saturday in *weekly* recognition of the resurrection of Christ.
- And nowhere did Jesus, or anyone else with authority to do so, command that the followers of Christ celebrate Christmas. It just isn't in the Bible.

Somewhere else in this book the issue of Christmas's combination—some would say adulteration—with non-Christian celebrations will be addressed. But right off the top we should look at what Christmas was when it was first devised or conceived, when it first began to be celebrated by Christians. More than anything, the original purpose or reason for such a celebration defines it. What is Christmas?

Two Christmas songs come to mind that bear the title, "Christmas Is." They list a number of things Christmas certainly *seems* to be about. One of them says, "Christmas is sleigh bells / Christmas is caring / Christmas is holly / Christmas is sharing."[1] The other says "Christmas is music and family in town / Christmas is Snoopy and Charlie Brown."[2]

Other Christmas songs through the years have told us that Christmas is snow and lights on trees and happy children.

Christmas cards feature similar sayings that purport to define Christmas, some of them generalizing in a very secular way, "Christmas is the warmth of home and the love of family." That sort of thing is the cultural mythology about Christmas. It's a fuzzy, imprecise, sentimental construct resulting from generations of celebration in an increasingly non-religious western culture.

We certainly see all those things and associate them with the celebration of Christmas; however, it's going too far to say that "Christmas *is*" those things. But it's also difficult to stay away from making such statements, because we like typifying things, describing them by their dominant characteristics. Perhaps we're not in terrible danger of misleading ourselves as long as we know, in fact, what Christmas is.

When we talk about what Christmas *is*, usually we use the phrase, "the real meaning of Christmas." Most church folks don't have a problem understanding what the real meaning of Christmas is. But since every year we struggle with our society and, to be truthful, with ourselves, to "keep Christ in Christmas," it's always in order to repeat the fundamentals one more time. *What is Christmas?*

It boils down to one basic fact: Christmas is the celebration of the birth of Christ.

Plenty of people who never take note of this fact nevertheless celebrate something called Christmas, a secular celebration that isn't about anything at its heart unless it's the generic idea of giving. But asked to explain why they celebrate giving, many non-Christians could not tell you.

On a radio program during the Christmas season one year, some "expert" was telling the audience how to celebrate around the office, and he recommended having a generic holiday, drawing names out of a hat, and giving a gift with no significance attached—whether Christmas, Hanukkah or Kwanza or whatever—and he said, "After all, good feelings and relationships is what it's all about."

Well, that sounds nice, but it's baloney. Whether people know or don't know the roots of the celebration, everything we have long associated with Christmas—Christmas spirit, giving, good will, charity, love, children, joy, peace—all derive from the birth of Christ. If there's anything Christmas is about, it's the birth of Christ. The core event was announced by an angel to shepherds outside Bethlehem, as recorded by Luke the evangelist in Luke 2:11.

For unto you is born this day in the city of David a Savior, which is Christ the Lord.

After he had given the shepherds some signs by which to find the baby, the angel of the Lord was joined by other angels, who said in chorus the words in verse 14:

Glory to God in the highest, and on earth peace, good will toward men.

Of all the events in history people might like to have witnessed, surely this would be a wonderful choice. The thought of seeing a host of angels lighting up the skies is thrilling. The angels praised God as they announced the gift of divine peace to people on the earth. And in the brief announcement they made, there was news of gigantic and sweeping proportions.

The answer to the question, "What is Christmas," from the message of the angels, is threefold: Christmas is an event evoking the praise of angels, demonstrating God's grace, and offering salvation to all people. Through your celebration of Christmas, you should experience God's grace and be certain of salvation in Christ.

An Event Evoking Angelic Praise

Few people have ever seen angels. The Bible is clear that they exist; in fact, they likely number in the millions.[3] They have been significant figures in announcing major acts of God to human beings. From the descriptions we have in the Bible, it is clear that angels perfectly worship and adore God Almighty. In the nativity account in Luke, a host of heavenly beings joins the one angel who made the announcement of Jesus' birth, and together they say (the Bible doesn't say they sang) words of praise: **Glory to God in the highest!**

The word "highest" is a neuter word in Greek meaning "highest places," and means the highest levels of heavenly abode. It is the place where angels reside and where the people of God who have gone to be with the Lord are. It is where God's throne is: the heaven of heavens. When the angels said, "Glory to God," they were inviting, even commanding, everyone in the highest heaven to give praise to God.

Angels are not incapable of sin: some did sin and became demons, we gather from the Bible. But those who didn't rebel and are still angels seem to be characterized by unswerving devotion to God, and are constant in their praise of him. Jesus taught his disciples to pray, "Thy kingdom come, thy will be done, on earth *as it is in heaven,*" and certainly this refers in part to the utter devotion of the angels to the worship and obedience of the Most High.

The birth of Christ was a event of awesome proportions, not only in our history, but in the realm of heavenly existence. That the eternal Word of God would become—not just appear as, but actually become—a human being, was an awesome thing!

By the way, the word "awesome" is thrown around casually today to describe the most commonplace things, but the incarnation of God the Son truly qualifies as awesome. It inspires awe and wonder. The incarnation had actually taken place nine months before, of course, when Mary conceived entirely by the Holy Spirit. But now the baby was about to be born. The angels were in holy rapture!

A minister hesitatingly risked telling a colleague something some readers may not believe. He said there had been a few times in his life when he had been in prayer and had begun singing, when he sensed in his spirit a chorus of angels singing in free form before God. He said, "I sensed an immense undercurrent of angelic praise going on. Whether they were joining me or I was joining them, I don't know: I suspect the latter. But somehow in my time of private worship I believe I tapped into the worship of heaven itself, and was lifted into that experience ever so briefly."

You might say it was the minister's imagination. And he admitted he couldn't be absolutely certain it wasn't. But he said, "The experience has helped deepen my own worship, but that certainly hasn't been my imagination."

Whatever you make of that report, there's no doubt that the Bible characterizes angels as worshiping God. When Jesus was born, their regular worship was multiplied, and they gave this exhortation to man: Glory to God! Worship God! Sing his praises! God has done wonderful and awesome things! The Eternal Son has left eternity for time, left the realm of the infinite for the realm of the finite. He has left behind his omnipresence to be one place only, left behind his omnipotence to become a human being, left behind his omniscience to start life as a helpless, innocent baby boy. Christ is born!

An Event Demonstrating God's Grace

Christmas evokes the angels' praise. One of the greatest reasons for their praise is that the birth of Christ is also an event demonstrating God's grace.

If you have read other translations of Luke 2:14, you have noticed that there are different readings for "good will toward men." There are some Greek texts (the better ones, actually) that have a single letter difference in the word for "good will" or "favor," resulting in a slightly different sense. The RSV renders the phrase, "peace among men with whom he is pleased." The NIV and other translations render it something like this: "Peace on earth, to men on whom God's favor rests." One has men pleasing God, resulting in his peace; the other has God pleased to favor men with his peace.

In other words, some people believe this announcement meant that God's peace on earth was for certain people, but not for all. But that can't be. The angel had already told the shepherds, "good tidings of great joy which shall be to *all* people" (v 11). God's good will is shown to all. Even if the original text contains the extra letter, the word "good will" must be interpreted in light of the rest of the angels' message. Therefore it cannot refer to men:[4] it must refer to God.

If human beings had such superlative good will for one another, one could make a defensible argument that peace on earth would not require an act of God. Peace, however, is the gift and work of God. The announcement clearly intended to say that God's good will was being shown in his gift of the

Prince of Peace, who not instantaneously but eventually would bring peace on earth. This peace would come first through the transformation of human beings through God's saving power. Jesus himself takes up residence in human hearts and brings both peace *with* God and the peace *of* God that spills over into human relations. And Christ will bring final peace when all enemies of his sovereignty and of the gospel are finally removed, in a day yet to come.

But perhaps in an even grander sense, this angelic word is an announcement of the act of God in demonstrating his grace to all humanity, regardless of the eventual acceptance of that grace by any of them. The fact is, God has been good to the entire human race in the gift of Jesus.

Again, this is true whether or not people accept the gift. What would the world have been like had Christ not come? Many of the hospitals and charities of the world have been started by churches. The great and continuing thrust of Christian missions is responsible for medical and humanitarian aid throughout the nations. Christian principles were behind the establishment of increasingly more democratic and less totalitarian forms of government. Simply the atmosphere created by an increasing segment of the population believing in grace, mercy, and forgiveness, has had an incalculable effect on the moral atmosphere of nations where Christianity flourishes. Indeed, in the coming of Christ, God has shown his good will, his favor, to the whole world.

The idea of "trickle-down" prosperity, or "supply-side" economics was the political talk of Washington back in the

1980s. The term "Trickle-down" first appeared in a column written by Will Rogers in 1932. Some pundits had a heyday with the concept. But recently someone in the media routinely ascribed the prosperity of a region to the benefits of the trickle-down principle. People have discovered that it does, in fact, work. One man's great blessing becomes another man's blessing, which in turn becomes another man's opportunity. And it trickles down, affecting many people. A rising tide lifts all boats.

Whether or not the American economy works best under a totally dominant "trickle-down" concept isn't the point. The point is that great blessings to all flow from singular, wonderful events.

God's great gift of Jesus was priceless, immense, enormous, monumental. As it has flowed down through history and across national boundaries and seas, it has blessed all humanity.

An Event Offering Salvation To All

But the point of God's general good will toward all men was that many would respond by welcoming the Christ into their hearts and lives, repenting of sin and turning the reins of their lives over to the Master. Christmas is this, too: an event offering salvation to all.

When Joseph was considering divorcing Mary discreetly, an angel appeared to him in a dream and explained why he must not: "For that which is conceived in her is of the Holy Ghost. And she shall bring forth a son, and thou shalt call his name JESUS; for he shall save his people from their sins" (Mat 1:20-21).

From the first, the birth of Jesus was clearly explained to be about individual, spiritual salvation. He was not just a great person who would inspire people to love each other: he was a Savior who would die for sins, rise to give new birth to new life, and command people everywhere to repent and surrender to his Lordship. He came to bring us salvation from the condemnation of our sins.

Georgia Knick Horne wrote a poem called "The Greatest Gift," thanking God for his gift of Christ Jesus:

The Greatest Gift

You ask what I'm wanting for Christmas,
　　What gift I would like to acquire—
A gift that would thrill my whole being
　　And satisfy every desire.
Well, just such a Gift has already
Been given—and it is my own;
For no greater love could be given
　　And no greater love could be shown
Than when God the Father gave Jesus,
　　His only, His well-beloved Son,
To suffer in my place on Calv'ry,
　　To pay for the sins I had done.

O Gift over all gifts transcending!
　　O Gift dear and precious, divine!
Unspeakable Gift God has given

To all who believe—and He's mine.
And since this great Gift I've accepted,
    To me God has given beside,
A life never ending, eternal;
    A promise with Him to abide.

He gives sweetest peace 'mid life's conflict,
    In days filled with peril and fear;
Gives joy day by day in his service;
    In sorrow gives comfort and cheer.
His presence is with me each moment;
    He satisfies fully my needs;
Gives grace for each test; bears my burdens,
    And gently my footsteps he leads.
What gift could I ask, then, beside Him?
    Could man such a gift e'er afford?
O no! God in mercy has given
    The greatest gift—Jesus my Lord![5]

The message Jesus told his disciples to preach throughout the world (Mat 28:19) was called the gospel. The word "gospel" comes from the Old English word godspel, from *god* (good) and *spel* (tale or news) and it means simply "good news." The Greek word ευαγγελιον (*euangelion*) in the New Testament is usually translated with this word. The disciples were to go everywhere telling people the good news that Jesus Christ, God the Son, has come to humanity, has died for their sins, has risen from the grave, and offers forgiveness and eternal life to people who repent of sin and surrender to him as Lord.

The good news is good because the bad news is so bad. The bad news is that "all have sinned and come short of the glory of God" (Rom 3:23), and that "the wages of sin is death" (Rom 6:23)—endless eternal death. The good news is that the gift of God in Jesus Christ is salvation from that eternal reality.

When the Titanic sank in 1912, it didn't have enough lifeboats to carry all its passengers. Some lifeboats had been removed to make the decks more spacious on the maiden voyage; no one thought they would be needed. When they *were* needed, some lifeboats were launched without being full—some were rowed away only half empty, and only after the ship went down did they return to the site to pick up additional persons. By then, it was too late. Other lifeboats launched full, and crew members in charge had to fight off frantic people in the water trying to get aboard, lest the small boats become overloaded and sink. It was late when the Carpathia arrived and took aboard Titanic passengers from lifeboats. All others had already died of hypothermia or had drowned.

If ever someone were needed to rescue the perishing, it was then. Now, we in the world, a world created by God for his will and pleasure, but diverted by our commission of sin, are perishing. We need saving. If no savior had come, generation after generation of human beings would be born, live and die and depart into everlasting darkness outside fellowship with God. But the Bible says that in the fullness of times God sent forth his Son, born of a woman, born under the law, that he might redeem them that were under the law—meaning that the law judged them to be sinners and the penalty of the law was death. Jesus came to save us eternally.

Can you imagine that anyone swimming in the frigid waters of the North Atlantic would *not* have grabbed at any outstretched hand, any thrown life preserver, so as to avoid drowning? It's equally difficult to understand why anyone would pass up the opportunity to have eternal life, when Jesus the Savior is offered. Perhaps it's because many do not believe they are in danger. Some don't believe they could ever sink, or that they will ever die, or that there is eternal peril just underneath the surface of the eternal waters. If not, why was Jesus sent to be our Savior? Why did he die? Why did he rise? Why did he send apostles into all the world to preach urgently that people should turn to God? Why?

The truth of sin's terrible consequence is the ultimate nature of the sacrifice made by Jesus. The Apostle Paul said that it's extraordinary for a human being to die in the place of another person, though some noble human being might dare to die for a good person (Rom 5:7). But Paul went on to say that God *proves* his love for us in that Christ actually *did* die for human beings, who are all sinners, deserving to die for their own deeds (Rom 5:8). Not only did Christ's dying prove God's love, it also proved that there was nothing short of his dying that would pay the penalty for our sins. If there had been something lesser that could be done, God would have done it. There wasn't. It took God the Son, becoming a human being in Jesus, born in Bethlehem and crucified on Calvary, to atone for our sins.

Christmas is the great event of God offering salvation to all of us through what God did in the Incarnate Son.

Christians, join the angels in saying "Glory to God!" Celebrate your salvation. And renew your commitment to serve the King of kings. What better way is there to "get ready for Christmas," as people often say, than to let God ready your heart and your whole life, for eternity with him?

2

The Challenge of Christmas
(Matthew 1:18–2:12)

For many people Christmas gets harder to celebrate every year of life. It may be the effect of aging itself. Growing older tends to result in declining interest in many things. Or it may be something about the age we live in, which seems to be marshaled against Christian faith and the mystery of eternal realities. Maybe the culprit is simply the classic enemy of the Christmas spirit: materialism.

A group based in Atlanta calling itself "Alternatives" (not now in existence, we think) carries on an annual campaign to get people to forego what they call "a spending orgy" and to give to the poor instead. The group's director talked about the tradition of great spending at Christmas and said:

> Churchgoers play a willing part...We are both victims and executioners in the matter of consumption. We are victims of a system that says the only way to live is to

consume, but we are also willing, joyful, participants in that consumption.

All this is true, and most preachers take some time every year to harp on it, hoping to make some impact on whomever is listening. However, preachers and other critics of Christmas consumption often oversimplify the "problem" with Christmas by intoning that word "materialism" and not thinking deeply enough to realize that for every one of us who is guilty of equating Christmas with "gimme, gimme," there is someone on the other side of the equation who is the giver. Where is the giver's materialistic and greedy motivation?

We could resort to the somewhat cynical argument that people give only because they expect they will receive, but that accusation broadly fails to credit the genuinely selfless giving spirit that motivates many people when Christmas rolls around. (And, we might add, if we indict givers for expecting also to receive, we have a problem with Jesus' assurance, "Give, and it shall be given unto you!")

Suppose, however, we accept the general truth of the premise that American Christmas celebration overall in the early twenty-first century, as it developed in the century before it, is dominantly characterized by materialism. Even if that is true, there may be a side to materialism at Christmas that most of us haven't thought of. If nothing else, it has become so incongruous with the message of the Nativity that thinking Christians have been *driven* to reexamine their part in celebrating Christmas the way they have done so previously, and almost every Christian has been compelled at least to think.

Sometimes your enemies do you a favor by making you strengthen your resolve. It may take a real threat by a real enemy to make you appreciate your homeland and your freedom. And it may take an extreme demonstration of greed and gluttony to make us realize how warped the remembrance of the birth of Jesus has become. If Christmas in the present day does this for Christians, it will have unwittingly blessed us more than it cursed us.

So, the world's distortion of Christmas challenges the church to purify its celebration. But let's not let the world put us on the defensive: Why don't we set the agenda for the campaign? We should be on the offensive. If anybody is going to challenge anybody else, Christians should challenge the world. It turns out that the agenda is already set, that there is a challenge. The Christmas message, as proclaimed by the Bible's accounts of Christ's birth, challenges the world at the point of its deepest needs and its most glaring failures.

The Challenge of Christmas is the standing order of the Christian faith, which puts the world on notice of the desire of God's heart: God wants us to believe, to care, and to hope. He is always trying to get through to us with this message, and the story of the birth of Christ is one of the most effective of all stories in communicating these truths. This beautiful bit of history confronts us with a set of serious challenges, and it will not let us go until we have dealt with them. It begins with a challenge to unbelief.

A Challenge to Unbelief

The world has stubbornly turned up its nose at the unpadded message of the gospel to repent and receive Jesus Christ as Lord and Savior. But it has been much slower in giving up its fascination with the birth of this same person. Maybe this fascination results from nothing more than the fact that most of us have a soft spot in us for babies. Maybe it's the quaintness or the pageantry. But whatever it is, God uses that fascination annually to get under people's skin and to confront them with their disbelief in who that baby was and what he did. Christmas is a continuing witness to the world that God so loved it that he gave his Son to save it. And Christmas challenges the unbelieving people of the world to break down and believe on Jesus Christ.

Actually, there are two kinds of people whose absence of belief Christmas challenges. One is (not surprisingly) nonbelievers—people who aren't Christians.

The Unbelief of Nonbelievers

The unbelief of nonbelievers is simply the initial resistance of sinners (which we all are) to believe that Jesus is their Savior. Many people in the world have never heard of Jesus, but there are millions who have, who simply have not made a personal decision to believe he is their Savior and to surrender to his Lordship in their lives. Looked at from the standpoint of God's sovereignty and the requisite work of the Holy Spirit to bring conviction, these are people who have not been brought to belief by the power of the Spirit of God, even though the gospel—which is the power of God unto salvation (Rom 1:16)—has been presented to them.

Some nonbelievers are profoundly ignorant of the Bible or know about it only from people hostile to it: friends, coworkers, professors, etc. Some nonbelievers know enough about the Bible to argue that Jesus was not the Son of God—often parroting other people without doing any critical thinking of their own. Still other nonbelievers simply ignore the question of who Jesus is and any discussion of the gospel. But the unbelief of all unbelievers is challenged by the annual celebration of his birth. In spite of the nearly overwhelming distraction of the secular side of Christmas, the core message of Christ's birth continues to challenge unbelief and to present Jesus as one who should be the object of our faith.

A boy growing up in Virginia read in the *Farmers' Almanac* one winter that it was going to snow the following June 7. All that next spring he kept track of the days, and told people it was going to snow June 7. Everybody thought he was crazy, but he explained he had read it in the *Almanac,* so it must be true. Come June 7, it didn't snow. It sleeted. Certainly, it was a fluke, but it happened. The boy figured the fellows at the *Farmers' Almanac* had a direct line to God. He was gullible, but for the credulous even a near-fulfilment is good enough! Recently, a newspaper story about the publisher of the *Farmers' Almanac* said that they buy their long-range forecasts from a company that has been producing such prognostications for years. The publisher said, "They don't claim to be accurate, and I have no idea if they are."

What that publisher really counted on was not the cooperation of the weather, but the predictable behavior of *Almanac* buyers, who tend to be a bit gullible anyway. The publisher said, "When we're correct, people say, 'Golly, you all hit it just right;' when we're wrong, they don't say anything."

The Bible's story of the birth of Christ challenges nonbelievers so insistently because of the fact that it takes place in the context of hundreds of prophecies about the coming of a Messiah. With the birth of Christ a lengthy string of events began to take place quite evidently fulfilling these prophecies one after another. Unlike the editors of the *Farmers' Almanac,* the prophets of the Old Testament were called and led by the Spirit of God, and their predictions were accurate.

If you try to make a case for the authoritativeness of self-appointed prophets, you run into all their failed prophecies as damaging evidence. But God-appointed prophets make predictions based on the moving of the Holy Spirit, and they always come true. Not one of the prophetic words of the Old Testament writers has failed, and not one will. Scores of identifiable predictions of the coming of the Messiah came true in the birth, life, death and resurrection of this one man, Jesus. A few predictions/prophecies remain unfulfilled and relate to the second coming of Christ, which hasn't taken place yet. Since they are all tied up in the same story, once you recognize the supernatural character of the fulfilment of the prophecies of Jesus' *first* coming, accepting the guaranteed fulfilment of the prophecies of his return is a no-brainer. It doesn't take someone gullible to *believe* in Christ: it takes someone gullible *not* to!

A young Jewish man was given a New Testament which he read very carefully. Afterwards, he went to his Rabbi and said: "I know we do not accept Jesus as our Messiah, but can you tell me what our Messiah would have done that was different from what Jesus did during his life?" The Rabbi had no answer. A Jewish-Christian in Jerusalem recently produced a video of himself interviewing a variety of people on the street, reading Isaiah 53, the chapter Jews will not read in their lectionary: it's too clearly about the Messiah who came: Jesus. Many of those interviewed conceded, on an intellectual basis anyway, that the passage did, in fact, describe Jesus.

This is not to say that there is any "magic bullet" that will bring conviction to Jews, or anyone else, when read or presented to them. Many people will continue to say No to the gospel even when confronted in a dynamic way by a fully prepared Christian. But Jesus did not promise us everyone would listen. In fact, his commission to his disciples was to *go and tell*. He made no promise that everyone who heard would believe. *Go and tell* is about challenging unbelief through the presentation of the one in whom unbelievers should believe, while repenting.

The Bible's illustration of this challenge to unbelief is in the record of the experience of Herod. Matthew 2:3 says that when the Magi came to Jerusalem looking for the one born King of the Jews, "When King Herod heard this he was disturbed, and all Jerusalem with him." One can understand why Herod was disturbed: he figured he had a lot of good years left as king, and he didn't want some boy-monarch to depose him or his heirs. But what about the "rest of Jerusalem?" What disturbed them?

Probably they feared because they could predict how Herod would react. When the mad king was upset, no life was safe. But what does this say about the news that the long awaited Messiah had been born? Doesn't it say that they didn't really believe the messianic promises? Real faith, deep belief, transforms fear into courage and overshadows one's concern even for physical safety.

The Disbelief of Believers

If Christmas challenges the unbelief of nonbelievers, surprisingly it also challenges the unbelief of believers. Many who have accepted Christ as Savior occasionally retreat from their deep trust in him. We believers, too, need this baby from Bethlehem to get under our skin, to disturb us if necessary, to cause us to believe more constantly and to trust more implicitly.

Before Herod was disturbed, Joseph was disturbed. Matthew 1:19 says, "Joseph, her husband, was a righteous man and did not want to expose her to public disgrace; he had in mind to divorce her quietly." Joseph was a devout Jew, as much a "believer" as one could be for his day and to the extent of God's revelation—until Mary's condition was discovered. Possibly, in addition to learning that Mary, his fiancée, was already pregnant, Joseph had also heard her claim that the baby was conceived by the Holy Spirit. It is all too easy for us to sit here and say he should have believed her from the first. Honestly, do we ourselves not initially resist believing God—frequently if not almost always?

In facing our troubles, trials, emergencies or long-developing crises, we often try logic, common sense, do-or-die desperation tactics, anything before simply believing God. His written word may give us the answer, but it may seem to fly in the face of the way others say the world actually works. What God seems to be saying may also seem to call for more faith than we have or think is reasonable to expect from us.

The Christmas message as it involves Joseph, however, is that God is full of surprises and must not be second-guessed or underestimated. Christmas says you may have thought that the answer to your problems was money, time, things, escape, or something else, but the answer is Jesus Christ. Christmas challenges you to believe in him.

A Challenge to Apathy

Perhaps the most noticeable challenge of the Christmas message is its challenge to human apathy. This challenge is as persistent as the tinkling of the Salvation Army bell in the shopping center. It is as unavoidable as the figures of indigent street people huddling against the cold. It is as in-your-face as the flood of pleas for charity that come in the mail. Christmas confronts apathy and challenges us to care about people in need.

Mary was almost in labor as she and Joseph came into Bethlehem for the census. The succinct narrative in Luke simply says, "She wrapped him in strips of cloth and laid him in a manger, because there was no room for them in the inn." The text does not mention an innkeeper, but if there were one, we have done one of two things with him: we have made him a villain for slamming the door apathetically in their faces, perhaps grudgingly mentioning the stable below or out back as an alternative; or, we have credited him with being a man who had no choice but to tell them his place was packed with travelers, but then going the extra mile to take them to his stable, where there was warmth, soft hay to sleep on, and, most of all, privacy. Either way you look at it, the birthplace of Jesus was, by any standard, substandard. Contrast the place of his birth and his sparing surroundings those first years with the visit of the Magi, who, Matthew 2:11 says, "bowed down and worshiped him. Then they opened their treasures and presented him with gifts."

All this says that he who was accorded less than the ordinary dignities by the uncaring was worshiped as a King by those who were discerning. Perhaps not so much to make up for the inadequate treatment of Jesus as to act in the spirit he inspires, we are challenged at Christmas to care about people who are in significant need. Christmas confronts a culture absorbed in the hot pursuit of its material success, and calls it to remember those whose poverty is, embarrassingly, perhaps a part of that success. And the challenge is not at all unsuccessful. People give to charities and come up with all sorts of caring projects at Christmastime as at no other time of the year. And, although there are some who do it to salve sore consciences, or for a tax break only, most people show a surge of genuine concern for others. Perhaps we can hopefully say that Christmas compassion is a reflection of the miraculous grace of God that can temporarily and partly affect even a world in rebellion and cause it to flinch in pathos. Without this general grace of God, the world would be an utterly miserable place in which to live.

Bruce Rabon, when he was the pastor at Commonwealth Baptist Church in Charlotte, NC, heard someone saying, "There won't be a Christmas for some children," a lament of the plight of unemployed parents who could not afford to buy toys. Rabon wrote in his newsletter column that week:

> To say there is no Christmas apart from toys is to miss the point of Christmas completely. If Christmas were dependent on the merriment and mirth of gift giving (and receiving), we would be "of all people most miserable." Thanks be to God: Christmas is dependent only upon one Gift, the Gift of his Son.

Rabon's observation makes an important point. Back during the 1980s (a memory that dates the author!) a caller into a radio talk show said we ought to remember the MIAs (service members Missing In Action) because "They have very little to celebrate at Christmas." These days, we might update our references and express our concern about victims of the September 11 atrocities. At any rate, the talk show host responded, "Very little? They have absolutely *nothing* to celebrate." The MIAs themselves are actually dead, in all probability. We assume the caller meant their families. All of us might be sympathetic with the spirit the caller expressed, and none of us would envy the MIAs or their families' situations. But to whom did the so-called "first Christmas" happen? It was to a conquered nation straining to be free, whose bold patriots died in the resistance movement, among whom there was much hunger, sickness and injustice. They may have had none of the usual things to celebrate; however, it was to them the good news came by angelic announcement: "I bring you good news of great joy that will be for all the people!"

It is this, the *good news that is Jesus,* that is the cause for celebration, despite one's surroundings. No Christmas for some? That isn't true if Jesus is known there. As long as he is known, there is cause to celebrate.

But here is the heart of this challenge to apathy that Christmas brings to bear on us: we are challenged to care not only about the physical needs of people but also about their spiritual needs. We are confronted not only with a hungry or cold humanity, but also with a spiritually lost humanity. For those who have not heard of Christ, indeed there is no Christmas. How much do we care about that?

John Sanford felt this challenge keenly and expressed it well in verse:

They Never Heard of Christmas

Why have we not heard of Christmas?
Why have you denied us light?
We who long have groped in darkness
Chained by sorrow, sin and night?

Why have you refused to tell us
Of this Son born from above?
Why have you withheld such tidings
Of God's condescending love?

When was it you learned of Christmas?
Has this story just been heard?
Can it be that God would send him
Just for you who hold his word?

Will you still deny us Christmas?
Will we still reach out in vain?
Can it be that we must perish
Never having heard that name?

All our fathers died in torment,
Racked with anguish, fear and pain;
Never knowing of a Savior,
Never breathing Jesus' name!

Hear the words of hopeless millions,
Dying where no light has been:
Won't you share this Christ of Christmas,
Let him save us from our sin?[6]

Christmas challenges Christians to care enough to share their hope with those who so far don't have any. And this is the third challenge with which Christmas presents us:

A Challenge to Our Despair

Christmas is hope in pageant costumes. Where Christ lives and reigns there is eternal confidence and never reason for defeat by despair.

Incongruously, there's a lot of depression around Christmastime. Could this be because everyone tells you to have a "Merry Christmas," and the very expectation makes the emptiness of the empty-hearted more painful than ever? More than ever, they need the hope that the Christmas message holds: that God has sent a Savior to take away our sin, to make life good from the inside, to give purpose in living, and to impart confidence when dying. It is a message that Christ has come to break the bonds of sin and enable us to live righteously unto God. It is a message that Jesus has entered our world to walk with us as our holy, heavenly company. And as such, it is a message that challenges the despair of people like you and me, and says, "You can hope again, because this particular baby was born."

A six-year-old boy tiptoed softly up to the little crib where his newborn baby brother lay. In his parent's language of faith, they had told him his brother was sent from God. He stooped far over and gazed down at him, and whispering expectantly he said, "Now, baby brother, tell me about God before you forget!"

One baby did come from God, and though while he slept in a manger he had only the fresh consciousness of a newly-born baby boy, he grew to manhood in constant contact with God. In a few years, he realized in the most natural way that his God was the Heavenly Father, with whom he was in perfect fellowship, and with whom he was uniquely identified.

One day he began telling us about himself, and why he had

come. He told us about God, with whom he was one, and how God loved us. He so startlingly challenged our stunted and distorted concept of God that we did away with him by crucifixion. But he rose up alive, and challenged even the finality of death. And he ascended, and began communing through his Spirit with those who believed on him. He has been challenging the world ever since: challenging our unbelief, our despair, and our apathy, but offering us opposites: faith, hope, and love. Bundled in the manger was all this challenge, in the tender limbs of a baby. And every Christmas, the challenge presents itself again, giving us still another opportunity to draw close to God.

3

Capturing Creation For Christmas
(Hebrews 2:5-16)

From conversations that take place every fall, there seems to be consensus that every year the Christmas season slips up on many people more rapidly and stealthily than the previous year. As the years pass, they seem to go by faster.

There may be a corollary of Murphy's Law involved as well. This "law," a popular statement of common wisdom, is quite old, but its modern form is essentially: "If anything can go wrong, it will." There are numerous corollaries, and one humorous one is: No matter how much time you think you have until Christmas, you really don't.

The more Christmases that pass, the more many Christians not only run into the problem of coming up short on ideas for unique and special gifts, but also have a certain amount of difficulty coming up with more ways to make Christmas the season they think it should be for themselves and their families. It appears to be generally true that if you let Christmas "just happen," it will take the form that everything around you gives it—and these days that form is commercial, irreverent, Christless, materialistic, and cheap.

If you want your perception and experience of Christmas to be different from that, you must work at it. And that means doing some thinking, some changing, and probably some enduring, because other people don't want you to be different —it makes them look bad.

Too many of us have been guilty of a crime related to what Mark Twain noted: "Everybody talks about the weather, but nobody does anything about it." Well, everybody talks about the commercialization and cheapening of Christmas (most Christians, anyway), but few people seem to be really doing anything about it. The author decided early in his marriage to do something about it in his own life and with his own family. While their approach to Christmas may not be radically different than the reader's, the few things they sought to change received a more than moderate amount of resistance from people whose views differed.

Why would someone else care, for instance, that at the author's house they didn't participate in the fantasy of Santa Claus? They shouldn't, but there was no shortage of people unwilling to live and let live. Instead, they meddled, insinuated themselves, and argued their case for the mythical Santa (not the actual St. Nicolas) or attempted to sabotage the author's fledgling new traditions. All he was attempting to do was to recapture the Christmas season for the glory of God and the honor of Christ, in his home.

The question has to be considered whether reclaiming Christmas for Christ is worth it. Is it?

Recently there have been some Christians saying that the Christian community should let Christmas die. As we've already pointed out in a previous chapter, Christmas isn't an ordinance of the church, and we would have a hard time showing from the Bible why we ought to celebrate it in an annual way. True, it has shadowy ties with some non-Christian events in history as well as some blatant elements of non-Christian symbolism. But most Christians who celebrate Christmas have a special feeling about this holiday. They can't quite explain it. It's more than just that they always *have* celebrated Christmas, that they grew up doing it; something *compels* them to observe it. And something in them finds distasteful the thought that they should ever throw in the towel to the world and give up the season simply because it has become more the fling of the world than the feast of the believer. What is it that makes most Christians tenacious about such a thing?

A Mandate to Capture

The urge to appropriate the world around us for a high purpose results from something that God put in us. Created in us is the need to glorify God. We can reasonably conclude that believers are under a mandate to seek to bring the things around them into subjection to the Lordship of Christ.

That's the thought of 2 Cor 10:5, where Paul wrote, "We destroy every proud obstacle that keeps people from knowing

God. We capture their rebellious thoughts and teach them to obey Christ" (NLT). This "capturing" is done primarily by proclaiming the gospel, but there is an arranging of things, a direction of activities, and an appropriation of symbols and customs and meaningful ritual, that help confront our world with the kingdom of God—at least enough for the world to be exposed through these things to the kingdom message.

One caveat for Christians is that individual human beings cannot be saved eternally by adopting some semblance of biblical or Christian morals. Nevertheless, the impact that Christian teaching and example has had on civilizations has resulted in a humanitarian culture that benefits the spread of the gospel, and promotes its acceptance. That's reason enough for Christians to try to capture creation for Christmas: to capture it ultimately for Christ.

Try for a moment to probe the significance of the existence of a celebration like Christmas, with all its varied customs and symbols. The development of Christmas has taken place something like the development of a coral reef. Over many years, many people, with no conscious plan unifying them, built the Christmas season to be what it is today.

It's interesting to ponder what urged on these Christians in bygone days. It seems apparent that Christians' acquisition of so many symbols, stories, rituals, and traditions in their celebration of the birth of Christ has been motivated silently and perhaps unconsciously by the desire to bring the world around us into a kind of structural harmony with the eternal word of God. It's almost like Christians across the generations have been capturing creation for Christmas, or certainly making a valiant effort to do so.

"Capturing creation for Christmas" has a challenging ring about it! Hebrews 2:5–16 discusses various sides of the matter of Christ's coming and his redemptive work, but one phrase there sticks out and prompts readers to look through the Bible in search of other phrases that make the same point. The remarkable phrase is in verses 7–8:

You made them a little a lower than the angels; you crowned them with glory and honor and put everything under their feet (Heb 2:7-8 NIV).

The verse is a reference to what God said at the beginning, "Let us make man in our image, and let him have dominion…" The words make this point: properly oriented toward God, man is to be lord of his environment. He is not only to till the ground and manage wildlife, but to arrange and control creation so that all glorifies God. We are, as followers of God, to capture creation for Christ.

The title of this chapter is "Capturing Creation for Christmas," not "for Christ." But the intended meaning is capturing creation for the Christ of Christmas, the one whom Christmas should honor.

Is this a worthy goal, or even a possible one?

A History of Capturing

That Christians, as redeemed people, do attempt to influence, affect, and possibly capture creation for Christ, is clear from a few examples.

When we select the choicest high hills and build tall-steepled churches in view of every valley around, what is it but an attempt to capture even the vision of every person and direct it toward God?

When Christian forefathers wrote into the U.S. Constitution that all men are divinely created, and Christian citizens later led the nation to adopt as our national motto, "In God We Trust," what was it but an attempt to capture a nation's future for the cause of Christ?

When Christians eagerly enter the television and radio marketplaces and the internet with the communication of the gospel, what is it but an attempt to capture and use every available tool, natural or technological, to spread the invitation of God to salvation?

Capturing creation for Christ is just another way of saying what Paul said in 1 Cor 9:22: "I am made all things to all men that I might by all means save some." The Christian who allows the Holy Spirit to be Lord of his public as well as his private conduct attempts to capture creation for Christ by using everything at his disposal for the same purpose as Paul's: to save some—any who will respond to God's good news.

Many, if not most, of our customs surrounding Christmas are examples of creation captured for the celebration of Christ's birth. The custom of decorating small evergreen trees at the Christmas season began in Germany. Solid tradition indicates that an English missionary named Winifred in the eighth century replaced the pagan worship of a sacred oak and the human sacrifice occurring on it with the adornment of a young evergreen tree, which he told the pagan worshipers represented eternal life.

While, in looking back, we might question whether or not we would have done such a thing, we have to credit Winifred. If the story is authentic, then here was a man who encountered godlessness in all its horror, and he had the audacity and courage to step in and rebuke the evil, also replacing it with a beautiful symbol to represent Christian truths. This truth-related significance is why the Christmas tree has survived as an element of the annual celebration.

Christians have a habit of appropriating the things that surround them, fitting them into a scheme that will point to God and salvation in Jesus Christ. Cultural practices and icons that are not inherently perverse or otherwise beyond redemption often can be "baptized" for use by believers in preaching or illustrating the truth.

This sanctification of the secular describes the development of our modern Christmas celebration. In fact, it was more or less the official strategy of the church in the middle ages as it established missions in new parts of the world. Pagan symbols frequently were re-purposed with Christian significance, such that when—as they hoped—the pagan roots were forgotten as the pagan religion faded into history, the Christian meanings (while sometimes thin or vague), would survive and enrich the Christian celebration.

Unfortunately, the secular world has learned to play the same game, only in reverse. Over several generations, business and popular culture have extracted Christmas from its sacred setting and created a parallel observance, co-existing with that of the church. The world has a holiday while the church has a holy day, and we call them the same thing, but the differences are vast, and the world's event may be eclipsing the church's. It has passed the point at which we can talk about "keeping Christ in Christmas:" He is out of it, as far as the majority of the world is concerned.

We must not delude ourselves on this point. The world has taken over Christmas for its own purposes. It began with the supposedly benign act of referring to Christmas as a season of good cheer and happiness for everyone, especially children. But it took the critical step when celebrities and the marketplace drew the conclusion that you don't have to have God or Christ to have good cheer, and so Christmas needn't be distinctively Christian.

A Challenge to Recapture

As a result of this revolution, the time has come for Christians to decide whether the modern celebration of Christmas is worth saving as a means of proclaiming to the world the entrance of God into human history by the incarnation.

A minister got a Christmas card from a Jew—not a Christian Jew, a Jewish Jew. Reflecting on the oddity, the minister said that it seemed rather empty and contradictory for his Jewish friend to wish him a Merry Christmas. On second thought, he admitted that while the real meaning of Christmas wasn't shared by his Jewish friend, the fact that the man expressed his well wishes on the basis of the "spirit of Christmas" said something about the impact Christmas has had on the world of nonbelievers.

But the whole issue of the world's secularization of Christmas is typified by the remark of a woman riding a city bus at the Christmas season. The bus had just passed a church that was beautifully decorated and had signs out front announcing various activities centered on the nativity of Christ. And this woman was overheard to say, "Well, I declare! It looks like the church people are trying to *take over* Christmas this year!"

Have things really gone that far? Is the Christmas celebration as a whole so Christ-less, so unattached to the original meaning in the secular mind, that people have actually begun to think that it is the *church* that is horning in?

Moreover, to be brutally honest, the Christmas celebration has always been plagued (from the church's perspective) with the pagan roots of the customs the medieval church attempted to coopt or absorb. Secularists argue that winter-solstice celebrations such as Saturnalia never really disappeared, only transmuted into a stream of party-oriented forms over the centuries. To a degree, this is true. The strategy the church employed as it moved into the pagan regions of northern Europe, attempting to make Christianity easier to accept, backfired on them, and by extension, on us.

47

In the Old Testament, the Israelites swept into the promised land but didn't altogether drive out the idolaters and their idols, and it came back to bite them during the days of the Judges and beyond. Similarly, the church that sought to accommodate pagans a few hundred years ago purchased an easier road for missions at the expense of being later infested with paganism so intricately intertwined in the culture that Christmas, as an example, may not be capable of being "de-secularized."

It may be more difficult than we imagine to capture Christmas for Christ again. Or should we say, recapture? We have no power to make people who don't honor Christ stop celebrating something called by his name but that isn't reverential to him. But perhaps recapturing Christmas has more to do with a thing called visibility—how visible will we be in our public honor of Christ?

Christmas is nearly universal in our culture, and the name of Christ is right there in the name of the holiday.[7] Will we grasp the microphone, mount the podium, call attention, wave our arms, and shout, "Look! Christ became a man to die for our sins! Christ was born that we might be born again!" Will we capture our creation for the cause of crowning Christ in full view of the world?

We Christians are thankful for the number of churches attempting to gain high visibility for live nativity plays on hillsides and in shopping malls. We rejoice in the composition of new music for Christmas choirs that encourages the return of the believer to a simpler Christmas—a Christ-centered one. We applaud the courage of some believers in ending customs that have emphasized only greed, materialism and shallow excitement, especially fostering these things in children. However, we need to do more.

We need even greater visibility in holding forth the message of Christ's coming to earth. That is, we need to do more *if* Christmas is worth saving. Do we think it is? Christmas is the birth of the only hope of the creation, the only one who can give people in this old, sin-battered world new and eternal life.

A Christian asked his son, when he was three years old, whose birthday Christmas is. The boy said, "Jesus.' And mine, and yours, and mommy's, and Granddad's, and Grandma's—" and on and on he went! He got that idea because at Christmas we not only give special gifts to God for missions, but we also give gifts to each other. And he knew that we do that when it is one of our birthdays. So the natural conclusion was that Christmas is all our birthdays. Of course, it isn't.

Or, is it? Isn't it the celebration of the one whose life in us gives us birth unto a life that will never end? In a real way, does not your eternal life, and mine, have a special birthday in the coming of Christ, who is our life? And doesn't that make it important to keep the day focused on him? Doesn't that make it worthwhile—if it's possible—to try to *re*-capture creation for Christmas?

4

The Simple Facts of Christmas
(Luke 2:6-7)

As dangerous as it is to tamper with tradition, it should be done every once in a while "under inspiration." During mental and spiritual preparation for Christmas, a Christian is likely to encounter for the umpteenth time written materials, devotional thoughts, Christian songs, radio programs, and even occasional television programs, repeating familiar Christmas themes —among them "no room in the inn." It's high time, however, to see that verse of scripture, and the related passages underlying it, in a new light. This reinspection requires a little holy, inspired tampering with the tradition that has made so much of it, sometimes with the effect of augmenting the Bible record.

It's popular, as we know, to fill in the "missing details" of the Bible account. We liberally adopt the narratives we have inherited, which include the abject poverty of Mary and Joseph, their lonely and difficult trip to Bethlehem from Nazareth, and their virtual homelessness. We also supply an innkeeper, bustling

Bethlehem streets, ugly or insensitive travelers, and other such information we think necessary to envision what happened at the birth of Jesus.

Consider the humorous lengths to which we have gone to paint a portrait of the Bethlehem innkeeper, in particular. (See the chapter, "The Innkeeper Who Was Not There.") All we need is to watch any church's live nativity scene. The innkeeper will almost certainly be there, and he will say and do things that we have invented for him. There is such a thing as legitimate "historical fiction," of course, but in the case of the innkeeper, his story gets preached from pulpits and taught to children in classes at church as if he were really in the Bible. He isn't.

The fact is, the account we have in Luke, which is the only account to give any details about the night of Jesus' birth and the circumstances of its being in Bethlehem, is extremely simple in its telling, and it does not imply much of what we have historically inferred. What it does say is clear enough, but we may have to scrape away some gloss that tradition and sometimes superstition have added, in order to get the full impact of the actual scriptures.

The heart of the story is found in Luke 2:6-7, and reads this way:

While they were there, the time came for the baby to be born, and she gave birth to her firstborn, a son. She wrapped him in cloths and placed him in a manger, because there was no room for them in the inn (Luke 2:6-7 NIV).

Now, the way we have told it, Mary and Joseph, a poor couple barely making ends meet in Nazareth, left their hovel of a home there and went to Bethlehem because of the requirements of the census. Mary rode a donkey and Joseph walked, leading the beast. They arrived in Bethlehem at night and went straight to the only or the biggest roadhouse or inn there. There they met the innkeeper, who informed them (most versions say gruffly) that there was no room, that they would have to find another place. If there was another place, they got the same reception there. Some believe that other patrons at the inn could see that Mary was pregnant, but none was willing to give up his place so this soon-to-be-delivered mother could have the comfort of the inn. Yet in a sudden, embarrassed, perhaps reluctant surge of rough-edged compassion, this innkeeper led or just pointed around to the back of the inn to a stable, where Joseph and Mary could stay the night. There, that same night, Jesus was born.

This is pretty much the tradition that everybody is familiar with. Now, let's tamper with it. And it definitely needs tampering with, because it's so precariously situated on top of a house of cards. Let's deal first with the nearly universal assumption that Mary and Joseph were dirt poor.

For a moment, let's play "Mythbusters." You're probably familiar with the Discovery Channel TV show by that name that ran for seventeen seasons. The producers billed "Mythbusters" by asking: "Exactly how hard is it to find a needle in a haystack, anyway? And can water dripping on your forehead really drive you nuts? Those are the kinds of questions, myths and urban

ᅟ

ᅟ

legends that are put to the test in this humorous series that seeks to find out which myths are true and which are not."

Just substitute a few other words in that description, like "how poor were Joseph and Mary," or "who was the innkeeper." We should bust a few myths about the birth of Christ.

Busting the Myths

First Myth: Joseph and Mary Weren't Dirt Poor

The author has to admit that it took him a while in life to come around to realizing that Jesus' parents weren't the poorest of the poor. The cultural narrative about Christmas is that they were nearly destitute. Many Bible teachers and pastors parrot the same line, entirely because they themselves have read it in their commentaries and they have never questioned it.

This idea has been around a long, long time. It's perpetuated in each successive generation by poets, dramatists, preachers and songwriters. One of the favorite short pieces of prose about Jesus often read at Christmastime is "One Solitary Life." Paul Harvey used to read it annually on the radio; that alone gave it a sense of authority. The opening line of that piece is, "He was born in an obscure village, the child of a peasant woman."[8] There it is. Jesus was dirt poor.

Everette Patterson, a comic book artist and illustrator from Portland, Oregon, drew a cartoon about the night of Jesus' birth. It depicts what the artist thought Mary and Joseph would have looked like today. It shows Joseph and a "very" pregnant Mary outside what looks like a convenience store, standing in the rain. Joseph, a blue-collar worker wearing a work shirt with his name on it, a backwards hat on his head, and unlaced work boots on his feet, is at a public phone, holding a phone book and probably talking to someone at a motel. Mary is sitting on a coin-operated, but out-of-order, child's riding horse, holding her pregnant belly, and wearing a hoodie that says, "Nazareth High School" on the front. Considering the circumstances, she's probably meant to be interpreted as a school drop-out. On the storefront there are posters: "Smoke WEISMAN Cigarettes;" "Starr Beer;" and "Save [something]." A neon sign, partly obscured, says, "Re-elect Herod Antipas." You can barely make out graffiti on the phone that says, "Zeke 34:15-16," and when you look up Ezekiel 34:15-16 it talks about the Lord's feeding his flock and seeking those who are lost. A newspaper on the ground bears headlines about shepherds and good tidings. In the distance behind the store is "Dave's City Motel," and a sign in front of it saying "No Vacancy," but also, "FREE HBO," and "NEW MAN_GER," with the middle "A" missing.

Cute. And some nice touches in the posters and other incidentals. But it's misleading in the main, because the artist presents the ever popular idea that Joseph and Mary were scratching out a living. That they were very poor. That's the first tradition we need to tamper with.

Before we do, consider other images we encounter in modern times. First, there's the shameless misinterpretation popularized since early in the twenty-first century that Joseph and Mary were refugees. This idea has been around a while, but it got extra steam when political conservatives in America began talking about stemming the tide of illegal immigration from Central and South America by building a wall on the southern border of the U.S. Suddenly, people opposing that solution rediscovered the Bible story they were previously willing to discount as fable, and political cartoonists and others began blasting the nation with images of refugees dressed like Mary and Joseph approaching Bethlehem only to find it surrounded with a wall—suspiciously like sections of the new wall that went up on the Texas-Mexico border during Donald Trump's presidency. In some cartoons there are signs saying that "no room in the inn" is part of a policy to "Make Bethlehem Great Again," or just, "Border Closed: No Refugees."

Now, arguably, once Jesus was born, and *after* two years or so had passed, the little family members *were* refugees when they fled Nazareth to Egypt to avoid young Jesus' summary execution by soldiers who killed all the babies in the region of Bethlehem on orders of Herod. But usually, when cartoonists and other self-anointed pundits assign refugee status to Joseph and Mary, the latter is still great with child as the couple approaches Bethlehem for the first time.

This tradition needs to be tampered with as well, and it isn't difficult to do. Some longstanding stories that have grown up around the Bible account in Luke (and Matthew, too, for that matter) and have woven themselves around in them like vines in hedges, don't have much or anything to back them up. Unfortunately, like those thorny vines, they are easy to identify but sometimes difficult to remove. But let's take a hack at it.

Lack of evidence

First, there is no evidence that Joseph and Mary were *dirt poor.* We can stop there and let you go look, if you insist, but you won't find any. There isn't really any evidence that they were just *plain* poor. It wouldn't be possible to exactly compare the economic strata of first century Judea and Galilee with twenty-first century America, but if we do so only roughly, we can be quite confident that Joseph and Mary were somewhere in the very wide middle class. At any rate, if there had been an official, government-defined "poverty line," they would have been above it.

Why should we conclude that?

First, Joseph was a carpenter. Carpenters were in constant demand in Joseph's day, as they *always* are. Joseph likely had his own shop: the references to him and later to Jesus as a carpenter suggest Joseph's independent business and Jesus' apprenticeship in it. Carpenters had to have specialized tools. They had shops to work in, if only additions to their homes. A carpenter would have made a decent living.

Further, Mary had made a previous trip from Nazareth to "the hill country" of Judah, where Mary's cousin Elizabeth lived. Elizabeth, you'll remember, was six months pregnant with the child who would be named John—the Baptist. Many scholars believe it was Hebron where Elizabeth lived. Mary wouldn't have traveled there alone. In all likelihood, Joseph went with her. He had the substance to make this trip and to leave his business for the length of it. If he had employees, that fact would further establish his financial security.

Mary, and likely Joseph, stayed three months in Hebron. How could Joseph leave his work for that long? He had the money. Or he had the employees, and the money. Or if Mary went with some other trusted person instead of Joseph, then Joseph may have had to hire someone to help him at home, his wife's being gone. However you configure the story hypothetically on the basis of *known facts,* you don't get an image of a poor family just scraping for a living. They weren't rich, but neither were they just getting by.

When Joseph and Mary went to Bethlehem to be counted in the census—and to register to pay taxes if not actually to pay them—Joseph again left his business. We can reasonably conclude they realized Bethlehem would be overburdened with other travelers having to do the same thing. But it would be unreasonable to assume they thought they would just waltz into a Motel-6 and find a room. We can be certain they suspected they would probably not find room in an inn. But we can also be certain they had enough money to afford it if they did find a space.

Even further, since we know they remained in Bethlehem for perhaps as long as *two years* after the census, it is obvious that: (1) Joseph had the ability to leave his business in Nazareth in the hands of others or to leave it entirely—close up shop—and not be destitute in Bethlehem; or (2) Joseph opened up a shop in Bethlehem and carried on his profession there.

The probability that Joseph was not poor makes the typical, traditional depiction of his and Mary's trip to Bethlehem somewhat dubious. For instance, how many thousand Christmas cards have we seen that show Joseph on foot leading a donkey, as we've already mentioned, with Mary riding side-saddle (usually without a saddle), as they trudge over the hills toward the City of David? Again, we need to tamper, specifically by asking the question Why?

Why only one donkey? Why not two? Why not more? Why even the *one* donkey. In fact, why a donkey and not something else?

Okay, let's stick with a donkey, which was a common beast of burden and travel. Joseph probably made enough to afford two donkeys, one for each of them, and maybe enough to afford another donkey, to take the provisions they might need for an extended stay in Bethlehem. Why don't we ever see that possibility in the paintings? Probably we don't because the first person to depict the story fixed the image of the trip to Bethlehem in the minds of Christian artists for time immemorial. It may be nothing more complicated than that.

It isn't impossible, of course, that Joseph walked and Mary rode a lone donkey. It just isn't in the text, and other facts suggest that the possibilities are wide open.

The bottom line

The evidence is sufficient to lead us to believe that Joseph was *not* dirt poor. There is *no* evidence, however, to suggest that he was rich—whatever that meant at the time. The best we can say is that he was nowhere near destitute as a general state of life. And that reliable conclusion puts the lie to much of the myth about his and Mary's hard-scrabble existence.

Another myth that needs busting is the myth of the innkeeper.

Second myth: There Was No Innkeeper

A fuller diatribe on *The Innkeeper Who Was Not There* appears in this book in another chapter by that title, but at the risk of a little repetition, we need to look at a short summary of the matter here, to launch us into the subject matter of the title, *The Simple Facts of Christmas.*

The language is very neutral here in Luke. There is *no* innkeeper spoken of, and none implied by the writer. Of course, you can speak in the broadest terms of there being at least one inn (there probably were more) and the assumption that inns don't keep themselves: somebody runs the business. But that's about as far as you can go.

There *was* an inn—that much is mentioned[9]—but no word about Joseph inquiring about a room. As to how he learned the inn had no space for them, Joseph may have heard from people coming out of Bethlehem that the inn(s) were "full-up" and he might as well plan to sleep out under the stars if he didn't have family to stay with. Or, Joseph may have entered the little town and summed up the situation himself, from the looks of things, and then headed for the first shelter he could find. The Bible does not say, and it doesn't lean one way or another. *If* there was an encounter with an innkeeper, he may have been the most hospitable sort of fellow we could imagine, who was simply in a bind because he really did not have a single space left for another traveler.

Commentaries differ on the kind of inn that is meant by Luke's reference. Some say it was the large courtyard type, with walls around, but not necessarily any roof, where dozens of persons slept for a night, with no privacy. Some say it was more like a downscaled Best Western, with individual rooms at least. (We should suppose, however, that given the geography, it would have been the Best Middle Eastern!) The fact is, we don't know. So we cannot firmly establish that there were any ogling patrons or any ugly people unwilling to give up their rooms. Some of our favorite carols and cantatas describe the setting graphically, and give homilies on their own non-canonical details. Sometimes our renditions of the account are more fiction than fact. All we know is that there was an inn that was full, and this fact led somehow to Joseph's finding much less in the way of accommodations for the night than we may reasonably presume he hoped for.

In fact, we don't know that it was for only one night, or that it was that first night that Jesus was born. We only imagine so.

Commentary writer R. C. H. Lenski says that the phrase in verse 6, "while they were there," implies that they may have already been in Bethlehem several days before the birth of the baby. This would mean they were in the stable for not just one night, but a number of nights—a week, two? More?

But let's not stop there. We don't know there was a *stable!* Very early traditions (which we tampered with to get *our* traditions) say that they went to a cave, outside Bethlehem, near the shepherd's field. Bible commentators point out, however, that the manger may not have been in a structure at all. All we have in the text is the manger, nothing else. We may think a stable is the most likely setting, because Joseph and Mary would naturally have gone for what was most private, but these details are not necessary. And this is *exactly* the point we should pursue.

The invented details are not necessary

We have added so much to the story of Christ's birth over the years, for the sake of quaint beauty, that we have often succeeded in obscuring its meaning under a blanket of fiction. The Christmas story is beautiful by itself, without embellishment, but even more than this, it is meaningful, and its meaning, not its beauty, is what holds the power to change our lives and lead us continually to God.

This was the purpose in our tampering: to establish the importance of getting whatever we get out of Christmas not from what we like to *imagine,* but from what the Bible actually *says.* And what the Bible says is quite sufficient to lead us to meaningful conclusions and applications of its truth without resorting to embellishment of any kind.

Now that we've busted some myths (only two, and there are others) about the birth of Christ, we should make several significant observations about this short and simple text in Luke. These observations make up a body of profound teaching in scripture that rises above the empty sentimentalism that typifies much Christmas lore.

God Chose the Humble Circumstances of the Birth of Christ

The first thing we need to settle in our minds is the matter of who was responsible for Jesus' cradle being a feeding trough. We are fond of indicting the elusive innkeeper for it (though some commentators give him credit for actually finding a warmer, more private spot for Mary and Joseph than the inn!). Some indict all Bethlehem for being insensitive and unspiritual. Some view the circumstances as pure coincidence, the unfortunate result of a Roman Emperor's decree. We should settle in our minds one thing: *God chose* the humble circumstances of the birth of Christ, just as he chose Mary to be Christ's surrogate mother, chose Joseph to be his legal father, and chose the exact time of his coming to earth.

Caesar, Joseph, and perhaps even an innkeeper and others were unwittingly involved in making decisions that resulted in the working out of God's foreordained plan, but it was *God's plan.* Bethlehem was the place he had his prophets proclaim as the birthplace of the Messiah, and he never planned for the Christ to be born with a silver spoon in his mouth. We have made the point that Jesus' parents were probably not dirt poor, but this troublesome trip to Bethlehem was by no means comfortable for them. And when Mary gave birth and used a feeding trough for a cradle, they were all definitely associating with the poor, at least for the time being.

Don't make the mistake of believing that Jesus had to be poor in order to relate to the poor, or to relate to us all. If you go down that path, you'll wind up having to accept the notion that he had to be a sinner to relate to sinners, and so on. In today's mixed up world, you can't relate to women unless you're a woman; you can't relate to minorities unless you are one of them; etc. The omniscient God can relate to anyone.

Nor was the manger (and, okay, a stable, if you insist) just a facade, an atmosphere of faked poverty for cynical effect. It was real hardship as long as it lasted. It was the result of overbearing rulers creating difficulty for their subjects, possibly either unduly or actually maliciously. Even if Joseph did have sufficient means, his resources were depleted unjustly by an oppressive government for the purpose of gaining tighter control of the people's lives and greater possession of the people's wealth.

Still, "no room for them in the inn" was God's idea, not ultimately a Roman ruler's. God wanted his Son to come to us in a setting of low estate.

Malcolm O. Tolbert gives this simple commentary on Luke 2:7, which says about all that's worth saying about the details before he gets to the heart of the significance of the account.

> The humble circumstances of the birth of Jesus are depicted in the story. The word translated inn properly means room. An influx of guests had preempted all the places in the room in which travelers slept. The parents of Jesus were required to seek lodging in the stable or perhaps even in an open pen. The first cradle to receive their son was a manger, a feeding trough. Thus did this "Man for others" begin his life. And appropriately so, for

there are no barriers in a stable. Superficial categories of race and class, as well as fussy notions about germs and dirt are unimportant there. All the poor, insignificant, forgotten people of the world can gather around the manger and dare to believe that the Babe who lies there really belongs to them.[10]

Tolbert dips into the popular tradition but mentions alternatives. His imagery is somewhat balanced. Note that he doesn't claim that Joseph was poor; he merely says that the circumstances of Jesus' birth were humble. What is important is that we don't add anything to scripture and make Jesus dirt poor just to satisfy some assumption of ours that unless he were, he wouldn't really be qualified to be the Savior.

People often misinterpret the scriptures in general to say that there is something inherently blessed about being poor. In spite of the fact that Luke 6:20 says, "Blessed are you poor," we have to realize that Matthew's account of the same pronouncement was, "Blessed are the poor *in spirit*" (Mat 5:3). And if you do a study of poverty in the Bible you will not come away with a theological principle that being poor is wonderful in and of itself, or that it qualifies you for leadership or greatness.

That said, Jesus did say that being rich was usually an obstacle to faith in God. Being poor often did tend to make people seek God for relief, for blessing, for the very needs of life. So, there's that.

But the bottom line is that some rich people believe in Christ while some don't, and some poor people believe in Christ while some don't. There's no rule, only a tendency.

The question is, did God's Messiah have to come as dirt poor (and remain that way) so he could be the Christ for the poor? We would have a very hard time making that point from the Bible without resorting to familiar interpretations and traditional imagery that have little evidence to support them.

God planned the entrance of his Christ to take place in difficult circumstances and humble surroundings, not so much to say that Joseph and Mary could relate to the poor, but that *God himself* comes in the person of his Son to *all humanity,* no matter how little of this world's blessings they may have. In essence, God used the humble setting as a symbol of the common denominator of humanity. Stripped of just about everything we can acquire in this life, it's just we ourselves who are left. When there's nothing to hide behind, to be distracted by, to depend on in futility, or to equate with our worth, we are who we are. We came into this world with nothing, and it is for certain we will depart from it with nothing (1 Tim 6:7). It is to the human being himself that God sends his Savior. God planned the manger setting to make this point.

Phillips Brooks' carol, "O Little Town of Bethlehem," emphasizes this same truth:

> No ear may hear his coming, but in this world of sin,
> Where meek souls will receive him, still the dear Christ enters in!

Most Americans, notwithstanding their various and conflicting political positions, were nevertheless impressed when they caught a glimpse of former President Jimmy Carter participating in a mission trip with his church from Plains, Georgia. Here was a man who was President of the United States, now swinging a hammer, sweating with carpenters and plumbers and ditch diggers to construct a church building in a mission area. We can assume he would have preferred not to have anyone call attention to his humble service. I'm sure he did not do it for notoriety, but instead because he wanted to serve his Lord. Even so, it was praiseworthy, as it would be for anyone who left leisure and comfort to perform such a service, but the praise goes to God.

Now, here is the Christ of God, who leaves his throne and his kingly crown to come to earth for us. And in Bethlehem's inn there was found no room. But that's how it was supposed to be! God planned it that way. It was just one more way God devised to present the message that Christ came to give life to the poor in spirit, to those willing to be humble in heart.

God Desires a Humble Welcome for the Coming of His Son

Having said that God planned the humble circumstances of Jesus' birth precisely for him to be available to all on a common level, it must also be pointed out that the fact that there was "no room in the inn" clearly *does* have some symbolic significance. It seems unavoidable that Luke recognized that significance, though he did not particularly indict anyone for rejecting the baby Jesus. After all, there was no full-page ad in the *Bethlehem Times* that day announcing the birth of the long awaited

Messiah. It is unfair to criticize an innkeeper or anyone else for not bowing and scraping. None of us would have done so either, knowing no more than they knew then. We cannot say that the residents of Bethlehem did not *care* who was being born in their town that night. The most we can say is that they did not *know*.

Be that as it may, the symbol of the inn with no vacancy and the stable of last resort was created by the providence of God as a powerful warning to us, who may easily fail to notice the approach Christ makes to us, or worse, deliberately shut him out.

This solemn reminder is well put by Norval Geldenhuys, who wrote:

> What the inhabitants of Bethlehem did in their ignorance is done by many today in willful indifference—they refuse to make room for the Son of God. They give no place to him in their feelings, their affections, their thoughts, their views of life, their wishes, their decisions, their actions, or their daily conduct. And thus they deny themselves the greatest privilege of all and incur the greatest loss to their lives."[11]

How true this is! Yet we should go further to say that what God wants of us is not only that we should *make* room for Christ, but also that we should *clear* the room for him. As somebody has put it, Jesus doesn't want to be first in our lives: he wants to *be* our life. This is hard for us, but it is the essence of the command of God. Yet, O how he chooses to say it! He slips quietly into the world through the portal of a woman's womb

THE SIMPLE FACTS OF CHRISTMAS

and the resting place of a manger, and softly seeks to melt our callous wills through the tender voice of Jesus.

God Seeks the Open Response of All People to His Son

What is important to God is not what we do at *our* initiative, but what response we make to *his* initiative. In the final analysis, we do not initiate anything with God anyway. This is the point of Christmas: *God* started something among humanity that brought redemption and eternal life. What God seeks is an open response from us all to what he has initiated in his Son, Jesus Christ.

Consider God's initiative and the response of people in the gospel accounts of the birth of Christ. God chose carefully and with great purpose the recipients of his announcements. Notice that he did not send angels to the gates of Bethlehem to herald the nativity. It wasn't that anybody prevented angels from assembling there or told them to go caroling on somebody else's corner. God simply didn't send them there. If there *were* bustling streets filled with busy people at that time of night, which is doubtful, they may not have responded with belief to the angelic message even had it been publicly announced. On the other hand, they *may* have believed—we just don't know.

The shepherds were busy, too, as we are specifically told: they were "watching over their flocks by night." Why make an announcement to shepherds and not the town merchants or travelers? We can guess at the reason. The shepherds were often despised by "more respectable" people, because they were not regular synagogue attenders, and because they were known for low-life ethics as a class. But God, who chose David the shepherd boy to be a king, knows men's hearts; these shepherds were open to what he wanted to tell them. When the angels appeared and spoke, what was the shepherds' response? They immediately came to Bethlehem, sought the child, and glorified God for the significance and the joy of the events of that night.

Nor should we read too much into the appearance of the angels, as if the shepherds had no choice but to believe. We make Christmas cards and tree ornaments showing little boy and girl angels and beautiful blond women angels, all with wings, hovering in the air, singing in perfect soprano a Handelian Hallelujah Chorus, when in fact the typical angel described in scripture appears like a full grown man, and has no wings during earthly visitation, but the chorus in the shepherd's field was evidently spoken, not sung (but, see the chapter, "The Songs of Christmas"). Still, it must have been a powerful encounter!

Yet many have gotten good news from God who have profoundly rejected or simply ignored it (when was the last time you read Jeremiah?). In the end, our response to God's message of Christ is up to us, and God does not *make* us rise up and seek Christ immediately. But the shepherds did just that.

Consider the Magi, over in Matthew's account. We have no word on their spiritual acceptability to the true God at the time they became aware of the birth of a king in Israel; some theologians speculate they were common astrologers and pagans, which seems likely. All we know is that they felt led to seek the child, and they brought gifts befitting a king. And while it is wise to note that nothing is said that implies that what they did in any sense "saved" them, it remains that their *response* is the significant thing: they came, they sought, and they worshiped.

However, consider Herod. He also learned of the nativity—second hand, but he learned. God may not have sent him an angel, but however the message came, it came, and at that point it was his *response* that became crucial. And what was that response? Instant rejection, which he attempted to cover up with a lie about wanting to worship him, and then an attempt to be rid of Jesus. One would find it difficult to maintain that Herod would have done anything differently even if angels had hovered over his bed at night and sung Bach's Christmas Oratorio. The heart of Herod simply shut out the spiritual message of God.

It makes no particular difference what our character is prior to our introduction to the good news of Jesus Christ. We may identify more with the hardened Herod than with the simple shepherd, or more with the worldly wise Magi than the pious churchgoer. But our past or our predisposition is not what determines our future and our relationship to God. What matters is our *response.* Whoever we are, whatever we are, God seeks an open response to his Son, an acceptance of him fully, as who he came to be. And on that point the angels left no doubt: "Today in the town of David a Savior has been born to you; he is Christ the Lord."

What Jesus came to do was to invite a response of repentance and faith in us toward him, but what he did to provide a specific focus for that faith was to die and rise again the third day. He died because when he grew to be a man, people made no more room for him than they did when he was born. Sinful man, devoted to himself, has no room for Jesus Christ as Lord.

But when Jesus rose again from the dead, his message was unchanged: Repent, and follow me. So the disciples went out to preach that the whole world was Christ's "room," that the kingdoms of this world are becoming the kingdom of our God and of his Christ. And in this kingdom, the roster of whose citizens is quickly coming to completion in this age, Christ seeks those who make all room, every room, available to him, by naming him Lord.

That kind of complete room is what Jesus seeks in our lives. That there was "no room in the inn" for him may have been everybody's fault in general and nobody's in particular, but if there is no room in *our lives* for him, there will finally be nobody to blame but ourselves.

One of the more theologically solid Christmas carols, which isn't as widely known or sung as others, contains a piercing message:

Thou did'st leave thy throne and thy kingly crown,
When thou camest to earth for me.
But in Bethlehem's home was there found no room
For thy holy nativity.
…O Come to *my heart,* Lord Jesus!
There *is room* in my heart for thee![12]

5

Jesus Was God's Idea
(Isaiah 7:14)

In thinking about Christmas you may realize how people acquire a somewhat contradictory mixture of the pressures of shopping, buying, going and fixing, on the one hand, and on the other hand the fun, beauty and joy of it all. And the celebration of the season seems to start earlier and earlier, as we've already noted. Some people suggest that as a practical rule, they don't want to see Christmas decorations, be bombarded with Christmas sale ads, or start hearing Christmas music, until *at least* after Halloween, and many people say it should be Thanksgiving. And we go through this routine *every year!*

But the other side of this is, we probably need Christmas desperately every year. Like the secular Christmas song says, "We need a little Christmas, right this very minute!"[13] Somebody wrote that if God hadn't come up with it, somebody would have had to invent Christmas, because we need a reminder of hope and an occasion of joy.

What God came up with, of course, was not Christmas but the birth of Christ. As we noted in chapter 1, *we* invented Christmas. The word simply means the "mass of Christ" (the Roman Catholic Mass) the celebration of Jesus' birth. God didn't tell us to have a birthday party for Jesus, not anywhere that anyone has been able to find in the Bible.[14] These festivities we call Christmas are our idea. But the thing that lies at the heart of our celebration, that gives it the joy and peace and hope that have become the hallmarks of Christmas, is something we can't take any credit for at all. Christmas may be *our* idea, but Jesus was *God's* idea.

One of the earliest specific predictions of the birth of Christ was spoken and then penned by the prophet named Isaiah. Just when the revelation came to his mind, we don't know, but he first said the words to Ahaz as recorded in Isaiah. We hear the words every year in the singing of the Messiah, in the reading of the Christmas story in its Old Testament context, in pageants and cantatas:

Therefore the Lord himself shall give you a sign: Behold, a virgin shall conceive, and bear a son, and shall call his name Immanuel (Isa 7:14).

Ahaz was king of Judah in a time of a menacing threat. Judah (the southern kingdom) had paid tribute to Assyria in 738 B.C., as had Syria and Ephraim (Israel, the northern kingdom), after the Assyrian Empire had swept through in 742. But now Syria and Ephraim had begun to plan a revolt, and wanted to bring

Judah in on it. Ahaz refused, and so Ephraim and Syria attacked Judah, hoping to overthrow Ahaz, set up a puppet king, and add a third country to their alliance, thinking they would be strong enough to stand against mighty Assyria. Ahaz had a choice: resist, or make a pact with Ephraim and Syria.

On the day this prophecy of Immanuel was given, Isaiah had gone out and met Ahaz by a pool at the northeastern side of the city of Jerusalem, carrying a message from God: 'Don't make these alliances: trust in God. If you don't, you'll fall.' As proof that this was God's promise and that he would fulfill it, Isaiah invited Ahaz to name some sign, any sign at all, that God would then do. Ahaz declined to name anything, so Isaiah announced one anyway, on God's behalf: a child would be born, named Immanuel, and before it was old enough to make rational, moral decisions, Assyria would crush Ephraim and Syria. The sign would validate this word of the Lord, that trusting in God's providence and power was Ahaz's only hope of deliverance from invasion.

This prophecy by Isaiah came quickly to mean far more than what it did for Ahaz in his own day.

The ultimate purpose of this prophecy's inclusion in the inspired word of God is for us to believe with all our hearts that Jesus Christ was born of a virgin, and that he is the only Savior of the world. The Holy Spirit's purpose in this prophecy is for this to be your personal confidence and commitment.

The ultimate truth that comes out of Isaiah's prophecy is that the virgin birth of Christ inaugurated God's personal presence with us and justifies our trust in him today.

According to this prophecy in Isaiah, God sent Jesus Christ in order to do two things: (1) To bring God's presence, (2) To save God's people. That was true for Ahaz and the people of Judah in their lifetimes, but in a much greater way for the entire world and the entire age.

To Bring God's Presence

Probably the most obvious thing about the promise of this special child Isaiah said would be born was the significance of his name. He was to be called 'Immanuel,' which means *'God is with us.'* In some unique way, the child was to signify the presence of God. How this presence of God would be realized is implied in the child's manner of birth: "Behold, a virgin shall conceive." To be born from normal sexual union says a child came from a physical mother and father. To be born from a virgin's womb says the child had to have come from somewhere else. That somewhere was from the heart of God.

People trying to weaken the interpretation of Isaiah 7:14 as a future prediction of the *virgin* birth of Christ point out that the Hebrew word translated "virgin" in Isaiah 7:14 is *almah,* and simply means "young woman." Their argument, however, is itself quite weak. In fact, it falls completely flat.

The Septuagint is the Greek version of the Old Testament almost exclusively used by Jews by the first century A.D. The Jewish translators of this version used the Greek word *parthenos,* to translate the Hebrew *almah.* The meaning of *parthenos* is specifically "virgin." The bottom line is that the word *almah* is always used to describe young women *assumed to be* or even particularly described as virgins.

It is this word *almah,* which could be taken in its barest technical sense of "young woman" but also as "virgin", that suggests to us the prophecy would have two fulfillments. The first fulfillment involved a young woman, and the second fulfillment involved a virgin. The first fulfillment took place in Ahaz's and Isaiah's own time.

Isaiah almost undoubtedly had someone particular in mind when he made this prediction. Some believe he was thinking of Ahaz's young bride and the heir she would bear. More likely, it was Isaiah's own wife who was to bear the child who was the first but lesser fulfillment.

Notice in the eighth chapter, right after the prophecy, Isaiah went home, and he and his wife conceive another child. They formally name him Maher-Shalal-Hash-Baz—How would you like that name?—but in a word from God in Isaiah 8:8, probably pointed at Isaiah's son, God calls him "Immanuel." It may even have been his nickname. Certainly he *needed* one! So he was a **type** of Christ through his nickname, even if it were used only on this one occasion. (A "type" in Bible theology refers to a thing or person that is a distinctive mark or sign of something else, particularly something yet to come.)

There was nothing miraculous about this first fulfillment of the prophecy. Its function as a sign was in the timeclock begun with the birth of the child: Syria and Ephraim would be crushed before the boy was eleven or twelve. In fact, they fell before he was three. God was still with Judah, just as he had said.

But Judah's history was to eventuate in a second fulfillment. It may be that Isaiah knew it would. Prophets usually have a much greater sense of the working of God than they fully explain to their audiences.

God revealed to Matthew, the gospel writer, that the major fulfillment of Isaiah 7:14 had taken place in the birth of Jesus. Mary, the mother of Jesus, was a virgin when she conceived, and continued to be a virgin until after Jesus was born. Jesus' birth was a miracle. He didn't come from man. Even Mary was only the host mother. The child Jesus was created within her fully and entirely by the Spirit of the Living God. God had become flesh.[15]

In Jesus, God is uniquely present in the world. Jesus came to do a specific redemptive work, but just the fact of his coming says that God is with us. That fact makes all the difference in our worship.

One Christmas Eve a pastor in Washington whose church was attended by President Franklin Roosevelt answered his office phone. Someone asked if there would be a Christmas Eve service. The pastor said that there would be, and the caller asked, "Do you expect President Roosevelt will be in the church tonight?" The pastor said, "I can't say. But I can say that God will be here, and his attendance will attract a reasonably large congregation."

It may well be that churches do too much entertaining, have too many famous people come speak, and depend too much upon the celebrity or notoriety of this present world for their hopeful success. What is needed is the presence of the Almighty God, and in Jesus, we have that presence. If the Spirit of Jesus

Christ, the Holy Spirit of God is present, we really shouldn't care who else is. And, if God is with us, we can manage anything we must live with.

Susanna Wesley, mother of John and Charles Wesley, was dying, and called her children to her bedside. She told them not to cry, but to sing a hymn, and to remember that the greatest comfort we have in any circumstance is the fact that God is with us.

Sometimes, presence is the most important thing. A pastor who described himself as majoring on "the functional," struggled with encounters where none of his ministry gifts was really needed. He sat with people who were going through great grief or trouble, and he said "I wished I could *do* something for them, but they told me there wasn't anything I *could* do. Just being there was enough."

In a greater way, that's what we need from God, and that's what he gives us. In Jesus, God gave us his presence, and even when he left the earth, he promised all his followers, "I will be with you, even unto the end of the age."

But presence isn't all of it. A minister sometimes walks from a death row cell to an execution chamber with a condemned man, just to give him comfort. But he can't save him. Fortunately, God didn't come down just to *be* with us, but also to *save* us.

To Save God's People

The whole thrust of Isaiah's word to Ahaz was that there was no need for him to go off doing something rash out of fear. Syria and Ephraim threatened him, but they were, as the prophets said, "smoldering stubs of firewood." They were practically gone out, finished, themselves. If Ahaz made alliances with them against Assyria, he would be finished off with them; the Assyrians would see to that. If he held fast, however, Assyria would take care of them in short order. In a way, the situation was like the cartoons you see depicting a little fish being chased by a larger fish ready to eat him. Only behind the larger fish, unknown to him, is an even bigger one, ready to eat *him*.

The sense of the sign of Immanuel was that God was at work through even the oppression of Assyria, and that if the people of Judah would just entrust themselves to God, not banking on human solutions, they would be saved from destruction.

It is this greater, universal, spiritual sense in which the sign of Immanuel has its utmost fulfillment. Jesus was sent to bring true and eternal salvation to all people on earth, beginning with the people of Bible history, and extending to everyone else. The angels who announced his conception said he was to be named Jesus because he would save his people from their sin. The angels who announced Jesus' birth said, "Unto you is born this day in the city of David a Savior who is Christ the Lord." God, in the person of the Word, became flesh, in order to *do* something very specific that would accomplish salvation for man.

It is for certain that we need that salvation. The peril we need saving from is our sin and its condemnation. We have left God. We have gone our own way (Isa 53:6).

The peril of man is this:
We disobey the *will* of God.
Therefore we deserve the *wrath* of God,
And experience *separation* from God.
If we continue without finding the *forgiveness* of God
And receiving the *life* of God,
We will live without the *peace* of God
And die without entering the *presence* of God.

The salvation of Jesus is this:
He who is the *Son* of God
Came as the *Son* of man, and
Died for the *sin* of man, then
Rose from the dead to be the *life* of man.
If you trust in him as the *Savior and Lord* of man,
He will save you from the *sin* of man, and
Grant you the *forgiveness* of God, and
Give you the *life* of God.

This may not be, in fact isn't, the way man would have accomplished his own salvation. Even the Jews took the law God gave, and made it into a way of salvation—or so they thought. They believed if only they could be good enough, God would overlook their sin.

People throughout the pagan world, then and now, believe that there are scales in heaven on which all their deeds will be weighed, and that they will balance out on the side of life, if only because they were sincere or because they didn't do something as bad as someone else. But that's not the way God works. And the way God *does work,* there was only one way to save us from eternal death: Jesus was that way. Jesus was God's idea.

There was nothing that could keep God from coming to us to save us. Man was not particularly united in the desire to be saved, or clear on how it must be done. But never mind, because God was.

March 11, 1942 was a dark day at Corregidor in the Philippines. War in the Pacific was bleak for the Allied forces. Finally the enemy marched into the Philippines. Surrender was inevitable. But the brilliant and bold soldier Douglas MacArthur had only three words for his comrades as he stepped into the escape boat destined for Australia: "I shall return." A little over two and a half years later, October 20, 1944, he stepped again on Philippine soil, landing safely at Leyte Island, and said, "I have returned." MacArthur kept his word, despite the power and strategy of the enemy. And because of it, an island was liberated.

How much greater was the victory of God, who by his prophet promised a little, beleaguered, and not even a good king, that a child would be born who would be "God with us." A whole world needed liberating, and when God, through this baby, stepped on earth's shores, salvation would have come.

Ahaz was not thinking too much about salvation right then. Isaiah may or may not even have realized exactly what the prophecy would ultimately mean. In fact, even when the second fulfillment of the sign came to pass two thousand years ago, the world was looking the other way.

In 1809, the world was watching Napoleon. Every eye was on the eventful happenings among kings and emperors. But all the while, babies were being born. In 1809, halfway between the Napoleon's battles of Trafalgar and Waterloo, William E. Gladstone was born in Liverpool, England. Alfred Lord Tennyson was born in Summersby. Oliver Wendell Holmes in Boston; Felix Mendelssohn in Hamburg, Germany; and in a little cabin in Hodgenville, Kentucky, a little baby was born and given the name Abraham Lincoln. In 1809 people's minds were occupied with battles, not babies. Yet, 181 years later, many people are vague on the details of Trafalgar, or even Waterloo. But of those babies, we know especially one of them, who became the greatest liberator in America.

So it was with Jesus. When Jesus was born in Bethlehem of Judea in the days of Herod the king, though messianic expectation was high, there was no banner headline that the Christ had been born in the city of David. Angels were sent, yes, but to a private audience of ragtag shepherds. A star appeared, yes, but only a few distant mystics interpreted its meaning correctly. Yet the child who was born that night had come to save the world.

And it was all God's idea.

It goes without saying—but we're going to say it—that because it was God's idea, it was a good one: repent, trust and be saved. That's still the offer Jesus makes to this world: turn from sin and every other hope, trust him alone through surrender to his mastery, and receive eternal life. It really isn't Christmas without it.

6

Are There Any Shepherds Here?
(Luke 2:15–20)

All kinds of people celebrate Christmas: people who are Christians and people who aren't; people who "do" Santa Claus and people who don't; people who like Christmas carols and people who don't know any; people who have children and people who don't; rich and poor; happy and depressed; old and young.

People also celebrate in different ways. Some people celebrate like the Magi, bringing expensive gifts. Some celebrate like the angels, with one carol sing or cantata after another. Some people celebrate like Mary and Joseph, quietly and with pondering.

Does anyone celebrate like the shepherds? Are there any shepherds reading this book?

The shepherds were people who were completely open and willing for the Messiah to come. He had been predicted by the prophets. During the intertestamental period the various prophecies coalesced into a fairly specific expectation that gave hope to a country that had been dominated by one empire after another. The shepherds were people whose willingness for the Christ event to take place, however they saw it, made them the ideal ones for the angelic announcement, and the ideal ones to be the first to spread the news. More of us ought to be like the shepherds.

Their story is in Luke 2, as you know. Here are the verses that tell just the part we want to look at:

> **When the angels had left them and gone into heaven, the shepherds said to one another, "Let's go to Bethlehem and see this thing that has happened, which the Lord has told us about."**
>
> **So they hurried off and found Mary and Joseph, and the baby, who was lying in a manger. When they had seen him, they spread the word concerning what had been told them about this child, and all who heard it were amazed at what the shepherds said to them. But Mary treasured up all these things and pondered them in her heart. The shepherds returned, glorifying and praising God for all the things they had heard and seen, which were just as they had been told (Luke 2:15–20, NIV).**

If we were to celebrate Christmas more as the shepherds experienced the nativity of Christ, we would be people of much more spiritual willingness than we often are. This willingness of heart and spirit is the quality God is looking for in the recipients of the Christmas message. It is a willingness to seek Christ, a willingness to believe God's good news, and a willingness to commit our lives to him.

People Willing to Seek

We don't know if anybody from the packed inn or surrounding Bethlehem came to the manger. Even if they had been aware of an event worth gathering to see, the walk for many of them would have been a matter of minutes. Those who are reported as having come—the shepherds—made a more substantial trip, emphasizing their willingness to seek the newborn Christ. If we were to include the Magi—they didn't appear in Bethlehem for perhaps two years, by which time Joseph, Mary and Jesus were in a "house" (Mat 2:11)—they made an even more significant journey.

Have you have noticed that the angels didn't tell the shepherds to "go," at least as far as our record of their words. They simply told them what they would find. But the shepherds went anyway. When the angels had gone away into heaven, the shepherds' natural response to the good news was to go see for themselves. They had been given a sign, implying they were to go. And they were quite willing. They were, in fact, excited about the prospect of seeing what had been described, knowing how important the child was.

Likewise, we ought to be people who seek Christ. We cannot seek him in a manger anymore, but we are to seek him as the crucified and risen Savior, as the ascended and reigning Lord, as the Spirit in the church and the Lord of the Christian. God has sought us out in Jesus Christ, but if we don't respond by seeking Christ in our lives day by day, we will not change, grow, or mature. Jesus said, "Seek and you will find." Jeremiah 29:13 says, "You will seek me, and find me, when you seek me with all your heart."

The Bible teaches that we are to seek the Lord. Finding the Lord, finding his fullness of life, finding the answers to life's challenges, finding the purpose of our being here, is not done accidentally one day while going about our self-centered routines. It is the result of turning our hearts toward him and looking to him for his word, wisdom, and leading, indeed, simply for his being and presence.

Margaret Clarkson waxed poetic on this idea in a hymn.

There Was No Room In Bethlehem

There was no room in Bethlehem
For Him who left his throne
To seek the lost at countless cost
And make their griefs his own.

But there was room on Calvary
Upon the cross of shame
For him to die uplifted high
To bear the sinner's blame.

There was no room in Bethlehem;
And in the world today
Men will not give him room to live

And bid him turn away.

But there is room on Calvary,
And there he stands to give
A home to all who heed his call
And look to him and live.

There was no room in Bethlehem
For Christ, the Prince of kings,
From throne and crown to earth come down
With healing in his wings.

But there is room in Calvary
For sinners to abide;
And all who seek will find a home
In Jesus crucified![16]

If we *aren't* actively seeking the Lord, aren't pursuing righteousness in him, then we ourselves are being pursued. We are the targets of Satan, who the Bible says "is a roaring lion, seeking whom he may devour" (1 Pet 5:8).

Dan Montano wrote in *The Economist* magazine in 1985: "Every morning in Africa, a gazelle wakes up. It knows it must run faster than the fastest lion or it will be killed. Every morning a lion wakes up. It knows it must outrun the slowest gazelle or it will starve to death. It doesn't matter whether you are a lion or a gazelle: when the sun comes up, you'd better be running."[17]

Spurgeon wrote likewise: "If you are not seeking the Lord, the Devil is seeking you. If you are not seeking the Lord, judgment is at your heels."

In the Christian life, it is not enough simply to wake up. We are called to run, to become more like Christ, to press ahead in godliness, to *seek Christ!*

Are there any shepherds reading this book, willing to seek Christ?

People Willing to Believe

The shepherds were also people who were willing to believe. They were willing to see what they were told they would see and to believe that it meant what they were told it meant.

Notice that the shepherds went expecting to see what they were told they would find, and returned saying it was just as they had been told. "Let's go to Bethlehem," they said, "and see this thing that has happened, that the Lord has told us about." They had no reason to doubt that they would find everything as they had been told. And after they had gone, sought, found, and seen, Luke says, "They returned, glorifying and praising God for all the things they had heard and seen, *which were just as they had been told."*

We shouldn't make the mistake of saying that they had no choice but to believe, or that nobody in their position would have been skeptical. Luke says that when they reported the word concerning what had been told them about the child, people were amazed: apparently there was an element of the hard-to-believe in the report. Besides, we all know that even the most obvious things remain disbelieved by those with obstinate hearts.

The shepherds were not gullible: they were full of faith.

There is a tremendous difference between the two things. Gullibility is the tendency to be easily fooled or cheated. Often, it's a tendency to believe anything that appeals to the obsession of human beings with mysticism, magic, and make-believe. Faith is vastly different. It is a reasonable and spiritually motivated acceptance of things revealed by the word or hand of God. God gave us every reason to believe that the child born in Bethlehem was and is the Christ, the Son of God, who came to bring forgiveness of sin and the gift of eternal life. He is still looking for shepherds, who will believe.

People believe in various ways. Some folks who celebrate Christmas don't really believe in Christ—not in any saving, life-changing way. They may believe he existed or even that he was a good man and a fascinating and memorable teacher. But they don't take seriously the claims of his dying for *their* sin and rising from the grave for *their* salvation.

In a pastor's column a few years ago, Dr. Stewart Simms pointed out that in the Dallas school district at that time, all references to "Christmas break" or "Christmas holidays" had been purged from materials mailed to schools and teachers. Instead, the materials referred to "Winter break" or "Winter holidays." But, the Texas State Department of Education still used the term "Christmas break" in its communiques. To solve the confusion in terminology, and to avoid the hassle of changing its materials, the Dallas district began to refer to "Christmas" always in quotation marks.

Said Dr. Simms in a newsletter article:

The "" suggest an apology for the season. Every time 'Christmas' appears like that, it means: 'Please excuse us, but this is a temporary yet sorrowfully necessary infringement on your right to be protected from religion. We don't know what else to call it. The popular term is Christmas. Of course that refers to archaic beliefs that are somewhat embarrassing to those of us who know better. We have tried to change peoples' ideas about this season by substituting other secular images, but the idea persists that there is a supernatural meaning to it. And of course there is that name 'Christ' attached. Until we can find another suitable term, bear with us. We don't want to offend anyone.'[18]

And you didn't know quotation marks meant that much! The pastor was right, of course. That's exactly what those quote marks mean. And the situation is even worse at the date of this book's writing. We are steadily and rapidly approaching the day when no one in any public job will be able to exercise his constitutional right to free speech or his right to exercise his religion. And it's not just the fault of those who *don't* believe, but of those who *do* believe but are frightened into silence by the threat of persecution.

Many people who do not accept Jesus as the Christ, the only Savior, are like Herod, who believed in the pit of his stomach that the baby was, indeed, the Messiah of prophecy, and it terrified him. He was like the demons, who James said "believe, and tremble" (Jas 2:19).

God is looking for people who not only will know in the pit of their stomachs that Jesus is the Christ, but also will trust him in the depths of their hearts.

Believing Jesus was born to be Savior, however, even believing it deep in your heart, is not what actually generates change in a human life. Christ must be received, and he may be received only if he comes as Lord.

Paul the Apostle, who crafted several short summations of what it takes to become a Christian, wrote in Romans 10:9: "If you declare with your mouth, 'Jesus is Lord,' and believe in your heart that God raised him from the dead, you will be saved." Salvation is a matter of surrender. Believing and receiving means acceptance of Jesus as who he is, which is Christ the *Lord.*

People Willing to Commit

If you're like one of the shepherds of the nativity, you're willing to commit yourself to Jesus Christ.

We cannot go so far as to say that the shepherds became instant and devoted disciples of Jesus. After all, he was only a baby at this point, and they didn't know the half of what he was going to do. But we can say that with the knowledge they had of him from the angelic message, and the experience of actually finding him, they gave themselves to what they felt was what God wanted them doing: they spread the word. That meant commitment.

Luke wrote, "They spread the word concerning what had been told them about this child." In it's simplest form, even before baby Jesus grew up and died and rose again, what the shepherds were doing was evangelism. They were telling the good news.

Evangelism is an activity that marks the committed. There are many half-hearted believers in the world, but you will not find them spreading the news of Jesus. There are many who claim to be Christians, whose names are on the roll of some church, but they are not performing evangelism. Evangelizing the lost, informing the uninformed, persuading the non-believer, is what the *committed* Christian does. Shepherds are people willing to commit. Are there any shepherds reading this book?

Don McCullough wrote in his book, *Waking from the American Dream:*

> During World War II, England needed to increase its production of coal. Winston Churchill called together labor leaders to enlist their support. At the end of his presentation he asked them to picture in their minds a parade which he knew would be held in Piccadilly Circus after the war. First, he said, would come the sailors who had kept the vital sea lanes open. Then would come the soldiers who had come home from Dunkirk and then gone on to defeat Rommel in Africa. Then would come the pilots who had driven the Luftwaffe from the sky.
>
> Last of all, he said, would come a long line of sweat-stained, soot-streaked men in miner's caps. Someone would cry from the crowd, "And where were you during the critical days of our struggle?" And from ten thousand

throats would come the answer, "We were deep in the earth with our faces to the coal."[19]

The essence of discipleship is obedience to Jesus Christ. What he wants are some shepherds who are willing to put their faces to the coal, their feet to the path of witness, their hands to the work of service, their minds to the challenge of thought, their hearts to the business of caring, their money to the investment of ministry, their very lives to the call of God. Shepherds are people who are willing to commit. Are there any shepherds reading this?

If you think you could be a shepherd, here's an angelic message for you. Unto you is born a Savior, Christ the Lord. You will find him as shepherds have always found him: as one of humble but supernatural birth; as one of perfect life; as one of sacrificial death; and as one of victorious resurrection from the dead. He is now at the right hand of the throne of the Father, but the Spirit who makes him real and present in human lives is here, all around us. He is waiting to enter your life and bring Christ as Lord into your heart. If any shepherd here will seek him and then say Yes to him, he will enter, take charge, and give you eternal life.

7

The Songs of Christmas
(Luke 1:42ff)

The most enduring feature of our Christmas celebration is Christmas carols. We have many wonderful songs composed just for this season. Most of us cannot hear their strains without *feeling* like it's Christmas!

Probably we would have hymns and songs about the birth of Christ anyway, but specific inspiration for Christmas carols took place in the angelic announcement to shepherds outside Bethlehem. By the way, the Bible doesn't say they sang, but only that they *said,* "Glory to God in the highest," but it was as much like singing as anything in the world ever was. And once we've had the words put to music in Handel's *Messiah*, or some of the other great songs of the season, we'll never be able to hear these phrases and *not* sing them.

The angel's announcement was not the first such *song* of Christmas, however, nor the last. There were three before it, and two after it, at least from the record of scripture. None of these was set to music, either, and perhaps it's a stretch to call them songs, but really they are. Songs are exalted words that come from the heart and transcend mere conversation.

Such were the doxologies and prophecies of women and men who were closest to the events surrounding Jesus' birth and that of John who preceded him by six months. Elizabeth, Mary, Zechariah, Simeon, and Anna all broke into virtual song at some point, as the unfolding story of Jesus' coming inspired their hearts with praise. Look at their words, that were the first *Songs of Christmas.*

Elizabeth:

God Bless Mother and Son

Elizabeth was the first to give us song-like words about the Christmas event. By angelic announcement and a miracle of God, she had conceived a child, to be John the Baptist. In Elizabeth's sixth month of pregnancy, Mary came to see her. Mary had just received a similar announcement from Gabriel, that she would bear Jesus. In Luke 1:42 Elizabeth first sees Mary, and begins to say, "Blessed art thou among women, and blessed is the fruit of thy womb!"

We might call this song of Christmas, "God Bless Mother and Son." Elizabeth certainly glorified God, but she did so by honoring her much younger cousin, Mary. She praised her for her belief in the Lord. Elizabeth might have been thinking how difficult it would have been for her if she were unmarried to be told she would be pregnant, even given the very different, and holy, circumstances. Zechariah didn't initially believe Elizabeth would have a child the *normal* way, since he and she were both well along in years. What if she had told him that she was going to have a child that was not his? Would he have believed she was pregnant by the Holy Spirit? Even if she believed it? Elizabeth knew this was Mary's challenging situation.

Whether this was in the back of her mind we don't know for certain, but it seems likely, because she said to Mary, "Blessed is she who has *believed* that the Lord would fulfill his promises to her!" (Luke 1:45 NIV, emphasis ours).

Elizabeth's song is about the wonder of the personal experience of God. It's about sharing the joy of others' encounters with the Lord, and about being moved by their testimony, and inspired by their faith.

Many of our carols do the same thing: they exalt the diligent searching of Magi, the humble belief of shepherds, the courageous obedience of Joseph and Mary. In the way they responded, we hope to find inspiration for our own response.

Mary:

Magnify the Lord Who Saves

Mary's contribution to the songs of Christmas might be called, "Magnify the Lord Who Saves." When she met Elizabeth that day, and Elizabeth broke into a psalm exalting her, Mary responded by saying, "My soul doth magnify the Lord, and my spirit hath rejoiced in God my Savior" (Luke 1:46-47). In these and the next eight verses Mary concentrated her song on the mercy and justice of God, who had decided to send through her own womb the Savior who was coming into the world. She saw her miraculous experience as her humble participation in the greatest of all events up to that point.

Mary's song is about the awe of being caught up in God's work. She knew what was happening was not about her, not about Joseph, not about Elizabeth, or even about John, who was yet unborn. It was about God's working, God's plan, and Jesus was that work and that plan. It all focused on the Lord.

For too many of us, Christmas and life itself are about *us.* How fulfilled we are, how happy we are, "how good a Christmas we had," how life is treating *us.* Truly we need to lose ourselves in the purpose of God, and get our eyes off ourselves. We need to sing more songs like Mary's, that magnify the Lord, and the Lord only.

Zechariah:

Praise the Lord and Bless my Child

The third song sung before Jesus' birth was that of Zechariah. He was mute, due to Gabriel's pronouncement, from the time John was conceived till his birth. When John was eight days old and they went to circumcise and name him officially, Zechariah wrote on a tablet, "His name is John," and immediately he was able to speak. And this is what he began to say: "Blessed be the Lord God of Israel, for he hath visited and redeemed his people" (Luke 1:68). And at the end of his song he said, "And thou, child, shalt be called the prophet of the Highest, for thou shalt go before the face of the Lord to prepare his ways" (v 76).

Zechariah's song could be titled, "Praise the Lord and bless my child!" It was about the exciting portent of Christmas: that God is up to something monumental, earth shattering, life changing, in Jesus, and that we are part of the excitement. There was only one John the Baptist, but all Baptists and all Christians can be like John: we can all preach Jesus. While the way was prepared for Jesus in the world by John, with every generation there come new people into the world, and each of us can be used of God to pave the way in someone else's life to see the need of a Savior and to believe on Jesus Christ.

Paul felt that excitement, and he gloried in the grace of God, saying in Ephesians 3:8, "Unto me, who am less than the least of all saints, is this grace given, that I should preach among the Gentiles the unsearchable riches of Christ." And Christ himself has given each of us the privilege of going out for him in the Spirit and power of the Lord to make disciples of all nations.

Simeon:

My Eyes Have Seen His Glory
After the first three songs, those of Mary, Elizabeth and Zechariah, Jesus was born. Then the angels said or sang, and the shepherds came and returned glorifying God for all they had seen and heard. Actually, we might have added their "song" to our list. And then eight days after the silent night of the manger bed, Jesus was taken to Jerusalem to be presented to the Lord. There Joseph and Mary met Simeon.

We don't know anything about Simeon but that he was an elderly man who had been told supernaturally by the Lord that he would see the Messiah before he died. That day he was moved by the Spirit to go to the temple, and there he saw Joseph, Mary and Jesus. Here's what he said, "Mine eyes have seen thy salvation…a light to lighten the Gentiles, and the glory of thy people Israel." Then he spoke briefly and cryptically of the crucifixion and resurrection.

Simeon's song might be called, "My Eyes Have Seen His Glory." It's a song about receiving true peace in the person of God's Savior sent to us. It's about knowing that everything God has promised, he will do, and is doing. Simeon would not live to see Jesus in his childhood or manhood. He would not see him followed, then rejected and crucified. He would not witness the risen Lord. But he knew generally what was coming, as he predicted it, and he was okay—he was at peace— being who he was in God's plan for that moment.

When we receive Jesus ourselves, we may not see the end of the age and the fulfillment of all prophecies for history, but it's okay, because we come to peace with God ourselves, and we know where we fit. We are confident about our own salvation, and we realize God is on his throne and his plan is being worked out in the world. For that matter, we know that even if we die before the Lord returns, we'll come back with him! (1 Thes 4:17).

Martin Luther King, Jr., in one of his last speeches before being assassinated in Memphis, seemed to realize his life was not going to be much longer. He spoke of the destination of equality and freedom that he wanted not only for Blacks but for people of all colors, and he said, "I may not get there with you. But I don't mind. I've been to the mountaintop. Mine eyes have seen the glory of the coming of the Lord." Our society has been slow to adjust to the principles in which even we ourselves believe, "that all men are created equal," but King had glimpsed the future, if only in the closing of the age, that held the righting of all wrongs, and he was at peace to leave this world knowing justice was around the corner.

Simeon's song was a message of this kind: peace and joy having seen the boy who would be the Lamb of God, slain for sinners.

Anna:

Thank you, Lord: I'll Tell the World

The final song was sung the same day, within the same hour as Simeon's. Anna, an elderly prophetess who stayed in the temple area constantly, came up to the family of Jesus. Her exact words are not recorded, but Luke gives this summation: "she gave thanks likewise unto the Lord, and spake of him to all them that looked for redemption in Jerusalem" (Luke 2:38). Her thanksgiving to God was followed by energetic and persistent witness to those who were open to the news.

Those who "looked for redemption" may refer to a group she kept in touch with, especially spiritual and expectant Jews, who may frequently have discussed messianic prophecy. Or it may simply mean that her conversation about the child she had seen was welcomed by people who were receptive to prophetic developments. There are always those who are receptive to prophecy, and those who aren't.

We might call Anna's song, Thank you, Lord: I'll tell the world!" It's about the missionary mandate of Christmas.

"Joy to the World," "Tell the Good News," "Good Christian Men, Rejoice," "Hark, the Herald Angels Sing," "Go Tell it on the Mountain," and similar Christmas carols are calls to evangelism and missions, based on the story of the birth of Christ. They challenge us to come and see, then go and tell. We are not to linger long at the manger, rapt by the tranquility, soothed by the surroundings, impressed by the pageantry, lulled by the loveliness, and then simply go home. We are to "Make known abroad," as the shepherds did, and to "speak of him to all," as Anna did. Christ was born for this. Christ was born for this![20]

There's a story of a Christmas long ago that has been told and retold. Every reader has heard it or read it. But it deserves another telling yet.

The year was 1870, the place, the outskirts of Paris, during the Franco-Prussian War. It was Christmas Eve. French and German soldiers were fighting for possession of the city. Both represented nations were known at the time for being God-fearing.

It was twelve below zero in the trenches where shells and shot were thudding and men were dying, on both sides. But as the darkness of that Christmas Eve approached, the artillery exchanges stopped. Rifle fire became sporadic and finally ceased.

A strange stillness engulfed the battlefield.

Suddenly a young French soldier jumped out of his trench, stood out in the open and began singing: "O Holy Night…" (in French, of course). The Germans were awestruck. When he finished, there was a moment of silence, and then another voice was heard, singing, "From Heaven Above to Earth I Come," in German—the Christmas carol by Martin Luther.

This timeless moment, lifted out of its own surroundings of battle and death, lasted only as long as the songs were sung, with a breath of quietness on either side. Somewhere in the depths of the evening, the moral night descended once again and fighting resumed. But for a moment, in a way that lasted a lifetime for some, the songs of Christmas caused men to transcend the mire of the world, to glimpse the joy of God, to long for peace on earth, even to proclaim to each other their hunger for the love of Jesus Christ to knit their warring hearts together.

With Elizabeth, let us bless one another at Christmas. With Mary, let us bless the Lord. With Zechariah, let us experience the excitement of God's working. With Simeon, let us be at peace, grasping the future by faith. And with Anna, let us tell the world about our Savior. Our personal testimony, the song of *our* lives, may change someone else's life, as they meet Jesus through us.

8

Jesus' Secret Identity
(Mark 1:24)

Many people have wondered why Mark and John don't have birth narratives. It does seem curious, but though they don't tell about the nativity, they do deal extensively with what is central to the birth stories in Matthew and Luke: Jesus' identity. In Mark's gospel, he often treats with great interest the matter of Jesus' identity, and what explained it.

Years ago, Bible scholars began to talk about the Messianic *secret.* Jesus sometimes told people to keep his identity under wraps. He healed two blind men and told them not to tell anybody. Others had a similar experience, and even his disciples were charged just after the transfiguration, with not telling anybody he was Jesus the Christ, as Peter had just declared.

At this writing there have been twenty-seven James Bond films; the first was in 1962. People love spy movies, secret agent stories, about people who travel the world on a mission, often adopting cover identities to do their work. Jesus was no spy, but in a way he certainly was an agent—an agent of God, on a mission to break the power of sin and bring the power of salvation through his own life, death and resurrection. For that mission he had to adopt, for a time, a certain secrecy, until his mission was guaranteed success.

But his identity was detected by some people anyway—some by the Spirit of the Father, but some by unholy spirits.

Mark 1:24 tells us of a person who recognized Jesus' secret identity and openly and loudly gave it away. Jesus was in a synagogue in Capernaum on the Sabbath. Mark tells us there was a man there who was possessed by a demon. And verse twenty-four says,

And he cried out, saying, Let us alone! What have we to do with thee, thou Jesus of Nazareth? Art thou come to destroy us? I know thee, who thou art, the Holy One of God.

Mark never refers to the birth of Jesus, but he certainly writes about things in Jesus' ministry that tell us what the birth stories do. Never one to waste words, Mark gives us the core of the gospel, which is who Jesus is, and what he came for.

This is the whole basis of our faith. We must have the right Jesus to have eternal life. If you have the wrong Jesus, you don't know the Jesus of the Bible, and if you don't know the Jesus of the Bible, you don't have eternal life. It's that simple.

So, who is Jesus? Pretend for a moment that we are in the synagogue and Jesus is there, about whom there is much excitement, but much secrecy, as to who he is. Suddenly, a demoniac blows his cover. Did you catch it? He told us first that Jesus is:

The Man from Nazareth

"What do we have to do with thee, thou Jesus of Nazareth?" he said. The demoniac knew something about Jesus, and it made *them* enemies. "What have we to do with you" meant, "What quarrel do we have?" The man knew he was full of evil and that Jesus was full of God, and that spelled trouble for him.

In calling Jesus "Nazarene," he showed us he knew Jesus' identity. "Nazarene" means "of Nazareth." He knew Jesus' background. The man in the *synagogue* may not have known, but the demon in the *man* knew very well, and knew what it meant.

There is a possibility that "Nazarene" was an updated form of "Nazirite," which was an Old Testament man separated unto God, like Samson, who had unique power. But Matthew's gospel specifically says that when Joseph, Mary and Jesus moved back from Egypt to Nazareth, it was to fulfill a prophecy that the Messiah would be called a Nazarene. This wasn't a prophecy in the Old Testament; it was probably a prediction known by the time of Jesus' birth but not recorded anywhere.

It's not surprising that either the possessed man or the demon possessing him should have known about a prophecy that the Messiah would be called a Nazarene, or that he should have simply known that Jesus was from Nazareth. What's surprising is that a man actually possessed by a demon should be able to go to the synagogue and not cause a stir!

Today, many churches exist that are so worldly that scandalously unrighteous people can even be members and no one cares. We should hope that in our churches, someone not right with God could not be in their midst for long before realizing he or she needed the cleansing and power of God, and beginning to desire desperately to be changed.

The demoniac may have infiltrated the synagogue, but he didn't attempt to deny that Jesus was the miracle worker of Nazareth, born as a descendent of David, born of a virgin, born as a fulfillment to prophecies that a messiah would come. Yet today, some people try to claim that there never was a Jesus. That's a fool's lie. But vastly more people try to ignore Jesus, *as if* he never existed. That also is foolish. When you die you will face him, as friend or foe. Better to receive Jesus now as Savior, than to encounter him later as Judge.

Jesus the Nazarene indeed has power. It is the power to save when you receive him, but it is the power and authority of judgment if you refuse him.

So, Jesus is the man from Nazareth. There's another way Mark's gospel identifies who Jesus was born to be.

The Man with the Mission

The demoniac said, "Have you come to destroy us?" The demon was speaking, of course. By his question, he reveals that the demons (plural) realized that Jesus' work, whatever it was, would threaten the powers of evil. Even a casual inspection of the history of the New Testament period reveals that there was unusual and intense demonic activity in it.

Indeed, Jesus came for this twofold purpose:

(1) To destroy the power of sin. The author of Hebrews says clearly in 2:14: "That by his death he might destroy him who has the power of death, that is the devil."

(2) To save the creation of God. Again, the author of Hebrews says in 7:25: "He is able to save to the uttermost them that come to God by him."

You are God's creation, but he saves *you* by destroying the work of *sin within you.* This is why he came.

Look closely at the word "come." This is the key word in Mark's account. The demon had reference to Jesus' coming into the world. In other words, he references Jesus' birth. The two most important points about Jesus' birth are who he was and why he came.

Jesus frequently spoke of his own purpose, and we should notice how often he used the word, "come:"

- "I am *come* that they might have life and have it more abundantly" (John 10:10).
- "The Son of Man is *come* to seek and to save that which is lost" (Luke 19:10).
- "I am not *come* to destroy the law, but to fulfill it" (Matthew 5:17).
- "I am *come* in my Father's name" (John 5:43).
- "For judgment have I *come* into this world" (John 9:39).

- "I have *come* into the world as a light" (John 12:46).
- "For this cause *came* I into the world, to testify to the truth" (John 18:37).

A long time ago in 1985 an ad appeared for a new baby doll. It was not your ordinary baby doll. It was a baby Jesus doll. It came in Anglo, Hispanic and Black models, and sported a glow-in-the-dark detachable halo and a price tag of $31.50 (More than $60.00 now). And it came in a wooden manger, with a card that says, "My name is Jesus. Jesus loves you. I am your friend. Please love me." The company that made the doll was founded by a Roman Catholic woman who said she believed anyone who was a Christian would want one.

Well, she could subtract one from her count. Another plastic Jesus won't help get the world any closer to salvation, or make it think any more seriously about the one who was born in Bethlehem. What *will* make a difference is more clear and forceful witness to why Jesus came, and what he wants with you.

Jesus did not come just to be a good influence, a religious icon, a charm against evil, or even merely to set the greatest historical example of love there has ever been. Jesus came to break the power of sin in your life, and to save you from it, by becoming your Master. He confronts you with your condemnation before God, and offers you the gift of life by his living in you. If you don't have Jesus, you have nothing to celebrate at Christmas. You can have all the toys—children's or grown-up's toys—in the world, but you'll have no Christmas without having Christ. He *is* Christmas.

The demons in this possessed man knew very well why Jesus had come. The difference between them and us is that we have the option of choosing to receive Jesus, while they didn't.

And if we receive him, whom do we receive? In the gospel of Mark, Jesus' secret identity is that of a man from Nazareth, and a man with a mission. But the significance of both of those roles rests on a third statement of Jesus' identity:

The Man from God

The last words the demon-possessed man spoke to Jesus were: "I know who you are: the Holy One of God." This was Mark's reduction of the essential message of the nativity: who Jesus is. Even the demon knew.

This name for Jesus is extremely precise:

- "*The* Holy One" means he is *set apart* by God above all others who may be called holy.
- "The *Holy One* also means he is the one who has the *Holy Spirit* "without measure." John the Baptist said this of Jesus.
- "*Holy…of God*" means he is the one who in his utter purity may be recognized as *God* himself in human flesh. It brings up thoughts of the *incarnation,* in which God poured himself into human flesh and became one of us. The baby born in Bethlehem was and is God the Son, the God-Man, the *perfect* one from heaven.

Those who say Jesus is just a good man or a great teacher

only, don't realize the importance of Jesus true identity, and in making such claims they cooperate with the arch-deceiver, who deliberately wants to conceal Jesus' identity from unbelievers. For the devil is a condemned being. And in response to God's judgment of him—which is unrelenting, beyond retraction, and ultimately destructive—Satan wants to destroy what God loves most in his creation: man. Satan does not want to help people, or fulfill their lives; he deceives people into following him so he can destroy them.

When Jesus came as a baby, Satan incited Herod to kill the babies of Bethlehem. Angels redirected the Magi and escorted Joseph and Mary to Egypt to protect the infant Jesus. Satan didn't get Jesus, but if he can convince you that Jesus isn't God the Son, or that it doesn't matter who Jesus is, he can destroy you. Jesus said, "Whoever believes in him (the Son) is not condemned, but whoever does not believe stands condemned already because he has not believed in the name of God's one and only Son" (John 3:17-18).

Marv and Marbeth Rosenthal released to the world without strings their poetic description of the identity of Jesus Christ. It may have appeared on more Christmas cards, have been printed in more newsletter articles, and been used in more Christmas sermons than any other poem in existence:

Mary Had the Little Lamb

Mary had the little Lamb
Who lived before his birth;

Self-existent Son of God,
From heaven he came to earth.

Mary had the little Lamb;
See him in yonder stall—
Virgin-born Son of God,
To save man from the Fall.

Mary had the little Lamb,
Obedient Son of God,
Everywhere the Father led,
His feet were sure to trod.

Mary had the little Lamb
Crucified on the tree;
The rejected Son of God,
He died to set men free.

Mary had the little lamb,
Men placed him in the grave,
Thinking they were done with him:
To death he was no slave!

Mary had the little Lamb,
Ascended now is he;
All work on earth is ended,
Our Advocate to be.

Mary had the little Lamb—
Mystery to behold!
From the Lamb of Calvary
A Lion will unfold.

When the Day Star comes again,
Of this be very sure:
It won't be Lamb-like silence,
But with the Lion's roar.[21]

And so...

Christmas is not anything important or joyful if Jesus is not the Holy One of God, if he is not the miracle working Messiah from Nazareth, not the Savior born to die on Calvary to turn men's hearts to God in repentance and faith. If Jesus is not the Christ, not the anointed one with the mission to save us from our sins, then Christmas means nothing. It ought to be eradicated from our culture because it deceives us into believing there is hope.

But there *is* hope: because there is Jesus; because Jesus *is* the Holy One of God; because he who was born and laid in a manger did come to destroy the work of evil and save to the uttermost those who come to God by him (Heb 7:25). Christmas is pregnant with this crisis and possibility: when you are confronted with your need of forgiveness of sin, and presented with the man Jesus, crucified for sin and risen from the dead, you can be born *again.*

9

The Innkeeper Who Was Not There
(Luke 2:7)

At a certain family's house during their children's growing-up years, they had a scapegoat, a standard, always-present personage who could be blamed, if only humorously, for everything that ever happened that nobody else would take responsibility for. Who broke the glass? Who left the door open? Who moved my things? Who spilled the water? When everybody denied being the one, somebody would suggest, "Maybe it was the little blue man who wasn't there." The parents probably came up with the name from a song from the Big Band Era, "The Little Man Who Wasn't There,"[22] and a 50s novelty song, "The Little Blue Man."[23] It was such a great idea to have a culprit so handy (who couldn't defend himself), that the whole family latched onto it.

Every year at Christmas we Americans—well, all right, probably Christians around the world—all hear about a little blue man who wasn't there. In fact, we blame him for some things that we regard as insensitive, to use the psychological buzz word of the past few decades. We blame him for being mean and rotten—and no, it isn't the Grinch. He's one of the characters of every Christmas pageant, usually the only villain appearing in these limited productions, if they don't go as far as depicting Herod.

We all know who it is: the innkeeper. He's the fellow who turned away a very visibly pregnant Mary, with the rude answer, "No room!" He's the one who made Joseph and Mary hunt up a barn to spend the night in. There's only one problem: we've made him up. The Bible never mentions him. It's very possible that in portraying him and frequently laying blame at his feet we are accusing *the innkeeper who was not there.*

Two previous chapters promised readers of a more thorough treatment of this rude, gruff, terrible, awful, malicious, unthoughtful, discourteous, rude, *insensitive* excuse for a human being later in the book. We have now arrived at the point at which we can look in greater detail at this character.

The only indication we have of a theoretical implication of a *possible* innkeeper is in Luke's birth narrative:

And she brought forth her firstborn son, and wrapped him in swaddling clothes, and laid him in a manger; because there was no room for them in the inn (Luke 2:7).

The discipline of Bible study should impose on every preacher, every Bible teacher, and frankly every individual

Christian, a severity that questions all tradition, all commonly held belief, all assumptions, no matter how longstanding. We should do this not because we want to be deliberately controversial, but instead because many of our assumptions come from inadequate Bible understanding. Many of our commonly held beliefs are colored by the culture around us or shaped by poor translation or poor comprehension of the original scriptures.

It doesn't take an expert in Greek or Hebrew to do this kind of Bible study: many study materials, starting with a reliable study Bible, can supply us with the tools to make good sense of what the Holy Spirit inspired to be written.

When we do this kind of rigorous Bible study, we have to come away from studying the Christmas story in Luke with some frank admissions about the innkeeper who was not there.

We Have Largely Made Him Up

Looking at the Christmas story, we should be impressed with the fact that there is no innkeeper mentioned in Luke, yet we have supplied all the missing details our pageant-oriented minds want. We have created a character who fits our expectations or prejudices, though perhaps not the Bible content itself. Let's look at the innkeeper who wasn't there. We may discover something that means more to us in the *real* Christmas story than the figment of our imaginations has represented in our traditional stories.

The innkeeper's existence depends on an implication in Luke, *if it is there,* that there was a particular inn to which Joseph and Mary applied for lodging. What does the Bible actually say?

The inn mentioned in Luke 2:7 is the Greek word *kataluma,* which is a flexible word that can mean any kind of place where one might stay, from a primitive inn, to a guest room of a house, to an unspecified place. The Greek version of the Old Testament, the Septuagint, uses *kataluma* in Exodus 15:13, translated, "holy dwelling." Luke himself uses *kataluma* in 22:11 to mean "guest room." In Luke 2:7, we have no other evidence to help us know what *kataluma* means. It may indeed have meant an inn, which was probably a road house, typically with an open courtyard where people could "bed down" for the night. Such a place would have a proprietor, an innkeeper.

Some Bible scholars, however, think Joseph, whose family came from Bethlehem, sought a place with relatives who lived there and had guest rooms in their house or houses, but he found that because of the census, all of them—there may have been quite a few out-of-town relations needing housing in Bethlehem—had committed those rooms to others. In such a case, there would have been no innkeeper to be encountered.

The bottom line is that we do not know. And our uncertainty is significant enough that we cannot honestly say it is *probable* that there was an innkeeper. The best we can say is that there *may* have been: Mary and Joseph *may* have sought lodging at an inn, *may* have spoken with an innkeeper, and *may* have been turned away. On the strength of that mere possibility, Christians have traditionally inferred an innkeeper's role in the nativity. And they have conceived of him in a number of ways.

Two possibilities have dominated traditional interpretations. A third may be surprising to you.

The first conception is probably the oldest:

He Gave Them Nothing

Most people picture the innkeeper as a gruff and harsh man who rudely turned away Mary and Joseph with little concern for what accommodations, if any, they might find. *He gave them nothing.*

This innkeeper was a man who had seen humanity from the inside out, run into every kind of character, heard every sob story, made paltry profit for his years of running a hostel, and developed a cynical apathy about most people. Never mind that such a man might not have stayed in business long with an attitude like that; this is the way most people probably picture him.

A judge active in community theater was cast as Mr. Potter in the stage adaptation of "It's a Wonderful Life." He determined to play the character three dimensionally, which in acting means as a believable person, not a caricature. He wanted the audience to actually hate him by the end of the play: only if they did would the plight of George Bailey be as desperate as it was. Every night of the run of the show, when the last lines were delivered and the cast came out for curtain calls, the entire audience broke into resounding boos when Potter walked out to take a bow. Then they began to applaud energetically. His portrayal was a complete success.

This three dimensional character of evil almost personified is the kind of person popular culture has made the innkeeper out to be. He's not some cardboard cutout, some mustache-twirling villain out of a silent movie whom readers are as likely to laugh at as to hate. He's a vile human being whose existence is commonly assumed to be obvious and whose actions are used to illustrate *authoritatively* the kind of behavior people should never imitate.

The Christmas hymns bemoan the humiliation of Christ, who was forced to be born in a stable and laid in a manger: "Such a babe in such a place—can he be the Savior?" "Away in a manger, no crib for a bed." "Thou didst leave thy throne and thy kingly crown when thou camest to earth for me, but in Bethlehem's inn was there found no room for thy holy nativity."

A story that's been going around for more than fifty years goes this way. A Christmas pageant was being planned for which a little boy had tried out for the part of Joseph but lost out to a rival whom he did not like very much to begin with. Instead, he had been cast as the innkeeper. The night of the play, he thought he would demolish his rival by changing his lines. (Every thespian fears people on stage will do that, because it often makes their *own* next lines meaningless, and they have to improvise.) When Joseph and Mary came to the door of the inn asking lodging, the little boy innkeeper, who was supposed to say, "No! No room!" instead said, "Sure! Come on in!"[24]

With his rival's reply, he showed why he had beat the other boy out for the part. He poked his head in the door of the inn, looked around, then turned back to Mary and said, "I wouldn't stay in a place like this! Come on, let's go around to the stable!"

Bringing this innkeeper into the twenty-first century for application, preachers, teachers and pageant directors, who put forth the innkeeper (who was not there) as a lesson for us all, chide us for not being receptive to the rightful Lord of creation. He came to earth to be born in our hearts, and like the innkeeper, many have turned away the gospel, the entreaty of believers to listen to the pleading of Jesus Christ to repent and turn to God. Christ asks to come in, and they give him nothing.

What's wrong with this lesson? Well, nothing. The lesson of the story of the innkeeper is true enough, whether or not there was an innkeeper and whether or not he was an old goat with no heart. The lesson itself, minus an innkeeper, exists already in the scriptures. For instance, John's gospel does not have a Christmas story *per se,* but in John 1:11 where he describes the coming of the Word to the world, John says, "He came unto his own, but his own received him not." As in John's day, the world is remarkably inhospitable to Jesus Christ in the twenty-first century, and it is getting rapidly and frighteningly worse by the day.

Another conception of the innkeeper sharply contrasts with the picture of a grouch:

He Gave Them His Best

How long this interpretation of the innkeeper (who was not there) has been around is uncertain. Its diametrically opposite take on the innkeeper is due almost entirely to the basic fact that there simply is no scripture to back up *either* interpretation: the innkeeper exists only in the minds of the interpreters. You see what you want to see.

What some others have seen is an innkeeper who was not a contemptuous lout, but was actually a kind man who immediately perceived Mary's plight, sympathized with her, and offered her and Joseph the best accommodations he had. In this scenario, he would have realized that a place along the wall of his inn's courtyard would have offered little to no privacy, and he lit on the idea of their staying in a separate stable, or in a cave, as one very strong middle-eastern tradition places the nativity.

In fact, a place called the Cave at Machpelah is identified to tourists of the Holy Land as a likely birth site, as an alternative to the other major site proposed by the early Roman Catholic Church. Anyway, this innkeeper, the kindly and helpful one, led Joseph and Mary around to this place, whether a free-standing stable or a cave, he fluffed up the hay for them, pledged to check on them to see if they needed anything, and he wished them well. *He gave them his best.*

Part of the reason this image of the innkeeper has arisen is a realization that a stable and hay might have been preferable to the crowded conditions of the typical road house. In other words, an innkeeper who sent Joseph and Mary to a stable—his own or another one—would have been doing them a favor, which he would have known. Such a man might have said (in this imaginary scenario), "Look, I could probably squeeze you in and make a few other people mad, but I have a better idea: I have a stable around back."

Another reason for the emergence of this interpretation of the innkeeper (who was not there) may be that we had rather create the idyllic image of Bethlehem's people giving their best to the Savior, even if it wasn't much. One of the Christmas songs that express that principle is "The Little Drummer Boy." All he had was his drum, so he played it for Baby Jesus. His "all-I-have" gift is revered, for the same reason that Jesus later praised the two coins a poor woman dropped into the treasury: "she of her penury hath cast in all the living that she had" (Luke 21:4).

In the spirit of "the best we have," the hymns beatify the manger scene: "All is calm, all is bright...sleep in heavenly peace." And baby Jesus is depicted as not like other babies: "The little Lord Jesus no crying he makes." Some even imagine that the cattle, sheep, and other barn animals gathered around to bill and coo over the Son of God, knowing somehow that they were in the presence of deity: "Man *and beast* before him bow." The pictures make it seem so serene and comfortable, when the reality was probably much different. It makes a nice Christmas card, but it's fantasy.

Nevertheless, when the lesson of this kind of innkeeper, who gave his best, is taught, we are encouraged to emulate him, to follow his example, and make room for Jesus in the best place of our hearts. We are reminded that Jesus himself tells us in Revelation 3:21, "Behold, I stand at the door and knock." Certainly we do not want to refuse him room.

It's not a bad angle on the Christmas story, and probably every one of us has noted it, and taken a lesson from it. The only weakness is in the idea that we are to give Jesus our *best,* when the Bible says we are to give him our *all.* To us, the word "best" or the concept of what is best doesn't always mean "everything." Jesus himself didn't choose the concept of "our best," but rather the concept of "our all" when he told potential followers what discipleship cost.

However, as long as we make the assumption that "best" means "everything we have, are, or do," we're safe in following the example of the kind innkeeper. Even if he never existed.

There is, however, a third possibility for the innkeeper who was not there.

He Gave Them What He Had Left

Suppose that the innkeeper (who was not there) was neither a gruff old man, waving away the hapless couple with indifference, nor, at the other end of the spectrum, a kindly saint who went out of his way to take care of strangers. Suppose he was simply a man who gave only what he had left.

This may be the most authentic image of all, if any of our ideas so far have any connection to reality. Here would have been a man who came to the gate of the inn and saw the woman "great with child." He could have made some attempt to find another customer who might be willing to give up his place. He didn't. He could have gone out of his way in some other way to help, but he didn't. He just gave them what was left. And in this scenario, he did so with relative indifference. Nobody else had wanted, or would want, to stay in the barn. It wouldn't inconvenience him or anybody else if Mary and Joseph did. If they wanted to sleep on the hay the animals had walked on, lain on and done other things on, that was their business. What could it hurt for them to stay there?

This image of the innkeeper makes for more useful application than any other. It hits close to home for multitudes of religious folks who have no room for Jesus in the center of their lives. They have no intention of giving him a place in the throne room, the living room, the heart of their daily activity or decision-making: they just give him what they have left. They give him the religious section, a diminutive little subdivision of their lives like a couple of bookshelves in a store or library, where they make space for some religious thoughts, some sentimental exercises in the family heritage, some learned, but awkward, prayers they hope will cover the parts of their lives they don't feel adequately in control of.

But what is troubling is that "they" are some of "us." We can *spare* $10 for a mission offering in honor of Jesus' birth. We can *afford* to give a few dollars every now and then to the Lord's work, because that's what we have left over. We have an hour left in the week after scheduling all our *real* priorities, and we graciously donate it to church.

Giving Jesus what we have left is what we do when we take care of our other needs and desires first, honor all our other obligations, exercise all our other options, do everything else *we want* to do, and then fit in church and the Bible at the tail end. What we have left may be a Sunday morning worship service once a week, or twice a month, or once, or a handful of times per year. It may be little more than a perfunctory check in the mail.

There are many "pretend" Christians who offer these tokens. In every case, those who give to Jesus only what they have left are concerned with symbol more than substance. Their greatest concern is to avoid inconvenience or sacrifice, while performing rituals that will give them the feeling that they are paying adequate attention to God.

Very likely, if the innkeeper (who was not there) had been hostile, Luke would have said so. If he had been especially gracious, probably the Bible would have given him credit. But that he is not mentioned at all may lead us to believe that if there *were* a particular innkeeper at a particular inn, he was just a typical, apathetic person, who did not distinguish himself by being either hot or cold in his response to the expectant couple who stood outside his lodging house. Instead, like many of us, he just casually pointed to what he had left over.

A terse little poem by B. P. Baker makes this innkeeper speak to us:

The Innkeeper

I only did what you have done
    a thousand times or more,
When Joseph came to Bethlehem
    and knocked upon my door.
I did not turn the Christ away
    with alibi so deft;
Like you, I simply gave to him
    whatever I had left.[25]

The Bible, however, does not chide the innkeeper (who was not there). It merely says they wrapped Jesus in swaddling clothes and laid him in a manger, because there was no room for them in the inn. That's all. Just the facts. We are forced by our own consciences to see the inappropriateness, the incongruity, and the disgrace of such a scene. Here is the King of Kings, coming to the land of the kingdom, and he enters the world with cattle feed for a mattress and the stink of a stall for a nursery. Welcome to earth, Immanuel. It doesn't get much better than this, and then you die, by crucifixion.

It is abundantly clear that God uses this unlikely birth for his Eternal Person to bring us to equal humility so we may see ourselves as proud usurpers, and then yield to the mastery of the Christ of Heaven.

There is no innkeeper to blame for inhospitable reception today; only each one of us. That verse speaks straight at us: "Because there was no room for them in the inn." May our tearful, broken, humbled hearts speak softly back to the Spirit of Grace, Come in, Lord. "My heart shall be Thy throne."[26]

10

Pondering Christmas
(Luke 2:18-19)

According to some studies, the old saying, "I'll sleep on it," bears more truth than might be thought. Researchers say that sleeping enables a person to set aside artificial stresses and sort out thoughts at a subconscious level. The result may be that after sleeping, an answer may come to mind that would not come before.

A retired man who developed the habit of playing Scrabble™ on his iPhone at night testified to the benefits of "sleeping on it." He said if he found himself stumped for making a good play, he would put down the phone until morning. When he picked it back up, almost always a good play would be readily evident that had eluded him before.

Whether your method is to sleep on it, or just take extra time to think, one thing is for certain: we all need to *think* about important things more than we often do. Some very important matters get awfully short shrift with us. Some matters of grave danger are waved aside quickly by the foolhardy, resulting in injury or death.

A news report described a woman who lost her temper in traffic, sparred with another driver, and wound up shooting her to death. What was she thinking? The fact is, she wasn't thinking. She was going on raw feelings alone.

People often give too little thought to the Bible, to church, to the gospel, and to spiritual things in general. Most of us are familiar with the statue, "The Thinker," by Auguste Rodin—a picture of it anyway. It's a popular and famous work of art. But thinking itself is not all that popular.

Thinking is challenging, and many do not want to be challenged. Thinking takes concentration, time, effort, and desire. Many people don't have such things to spare, they *think,* so thoroughly filled are their lives with other pursuits, many of them frivolous and ultimately unimportant.

Yet one of the things we are called to do as believers is to think, to consider, to ponder our faith, to meditate on the great acts of God.

Consider these biblical exhortations to think:

Romans 12:3:   "Think soberly, according as God hath dealt to every man the measure of faith."

Philippians 4:8:   "If there be any virtue, and if there be any praise, think on these things."

Proverbs 23:7:   "For as he thinketh in his heart, so is he."

Matthew 22:42:   "What think ye of Christ?"

Proverbs 4:26:   "Ponder the path of thy feet, and let all thy

	ways be established."
Job 37:14:	"Hearken unto this, O Job, stand still, and consider the wondrous works of God."
Psalm 119:95:	"I will consider thy testimonies."
Isaiah 1:3:	"The ox knoweth his owner, and the ass his master's crib: but Israel doth not know, my people doth not consider."
Daniel 9:23:	"Understand the matter, and consider the vision."
Psalm 1:2:	"His delight is in the law of the Lord; and in his law doth he meditate day and night."
Psalm 77:12:	"I will meditate also of all thy work."
Psalm 119:15:	"I will meditate in thy precepts, and have respect unto thy ways."
Psalm 119:148:	"Mine eyes prevent the night watches, that I might meditate in thy word."
Psalm 143:5:	"I remember the days of old; I meditate on all thy works; I muse on the work of thy hands."
1 Timothy 4:15:	"Meditate upon these things; give thyself wholly to them; that thy profiting may appear to all."

All these scriptures tell us the importance of deep thinking, of sober consideration of God, his revelation, his wisdom, and the meaning and significance of our lives.

Not that we always understand everything we think about. There are things we may think about for years, and never quite plumb fully. But part of our challenge is to keep thinking, keep piecing together the puzzle, keep comparing one thought with another and one event with another, and keep praying for wisdom, until God shows us the truth we seek.

If ever there were a time for thinking and considering, for wondering about the revelation of God, it was the night Jesus was born. After the shepherds had been told of Jesus' birth in nearby Bethlehem and had gone to find the child, they left, making known to everyone they met "the saying which was told them concerning this child." In other words, they relayed what the angels said: "a Savior, Christ the Lord," the message that Jesus, born that night, was the Messiah. The response of the people who heard ran the gamut from amazement to quiet contemplation. Luke 2:18-19 says:

> **And all they that heard it wondered at those things which were told them by the shepherds.**
> **But Mary kept all these things, and pondered them in her heart.**

When Christmas Day is past and January 1 is upon us, we often think about the opportunity of a new year. Sometimes people assign a special, periodic opportunity to the turn of a new decade. And when the calendar turned from 1999 to 2000 some years ago, a lot of people celebrated it as if it were extraordinarily phenomenal. In reality, of course, January 1 is exactly like December 31 most of the time. Nothing new really begins then except the calender numbers, unless people make it happen. One thing is certain, however: once Christmas is over, it fades quickly from people's memories. As someone said, Nothing is ever more *over* than Christmas. The sudden deflation of the emotional balloon of Christmas expectancy that takes place on December 26 witnesses to how little it really means to many people in the first place.

Instead, why don't Christians make up their minds to ponder Christmas a bit while it's going on, something like the shepherds must have done as they went back to their sheep, and what others they told about Jesus must have done as they made their way through the lanes of Bethlehem, and what Mary did, as she lay beside Jesus in the rustling hay.

Ponder Christ's birth a bit.

Something Amazing

Can you imagine the people the shepherds met on their way out from where the baby lay in the stable (or whatever it was—there's nothing in the Bible about a stable any more than there is about an innkeeper)? We've just "mythbusted" the innkeeper and some other embellishments to the Christmas story. But as long as we're dipping into the creative pageantry of Christmas, let's indulge ourselves in a little *historical fiction,* admitting to ourselves that we're embellishing, just for a moment. (Don't anyone put down this book and tell anyone else that the author thinks the following scenario actually took place.) Let's imagine the shepherds meet a trio of friends from their neighborhood. Matthias and Joses are the two shepherds and their neighbors are Amiel, Jonah and Ephraim. The scene is set just on the edge of Bethlehem, and here's how the conversation may have gone:

"Amiel! Jonah! Ephraim! You'll never guess what we have seen!" said Matthias.

"Don't make us guess, I don't like guessing," said Jonah.

" Angels!" said Matthias.

"Yes, Angels," said Joses.

"I'll tell them, Joses! Angels! Out in the pasture. There were scores of them!"

"One great one—he was the one who told us about the Messiah—" said Joses.

"Wait, the Messiah, what's this?" said Ephraim.

"Yes, *mashiach,* he's been born!" said Matthias.

"How do you know? Where?" said Amiel, Jonah and Ephraim, together.

"That's what we're trying to tell you," said Matthias. "The angels said he was born right here in Bethlehem!"

"And we've seen him!" said Joses.

"I'll tell them, Joses! We've seen him—" said Matthias.

"Yes, and you'll never guess where—"

"Matthias, just *tell me!*" said Amiel.

"In a manger," said Matthias.

"A manger! A manger?"

"Yes, the inns are all full. His mother gave birth in a stable, just over—over there!" said Matthias, figuring out the direction and then pointing.

"Wait a minute," said Jonah. "How do you know this is the messiah? What have you been drinking?"

"The angel told us we would find a baby wrapped up in cloths and lying in a manger," said Joses.

"That doesn't prove—" said Jonah.

"Ephraim," said Matthias, "how many babies do you think there are lying in mangers in Bethlehem tonight?"

"Good point," said Ephraim. "My heavens—Oh, my—do you think it could be true?"

"Are you listening?" said Matthias. "They were *angels!* They lit up the sky! They shouted praise, and announced the messiah's birth!"

"Yeah!" said Joses. "What's to wonder? What's to doubt! The messiah is born!"

And the shepherds go on their way, looking for someone else to tell, while the friends stand there in the way, their mouths agape, quizzing themselves as to whether or not it really could be true.

The Bible says "all they that heard it wondered at those things which were told them." This word "wonder" is a word that Luke used thirteen times in his gospel: *ethaumasan*. He liked it. It is picturesque. It means "amazed," especially in the sense of "awed" or "impressed." They were full of wondering anticipation about the import of what they had been told.

Are you impressed or amazed by anything these days? Many people aren't. We live in an age of wonders—technological ones, especially. We have put people on the moon. We have telescopes in space that can take detailed photographs of nebulae billions and billions of miles away. We have put a rover on Mars and sent home pictures that look like snapshots in your back yard. We have computers smaller than your fingernails, storage space for multiple encyclopedias on semiconductor chips smaller than the head of a tack, and we can transmit reams of information over fiber optics or through the air in a fraction of a second. We all carry around with us handheld devices that connect us to business, banking, entertainment and each other, that allow us to take high quality photographs and movies, and that enable us to see what's happening in real time all over the nation and the world.

To protect ourselves from being constantly stunned, we've turned off our amazement, and we take it all in stride.

But what if we were to hear that the God who made the seemingly infinite universe had made himself into one of his creatures? What if we were to hear that God, the person of his Eternal Word, had himself born into a young couple's modest home over in a nearby town? What if the evidence we were offered for this was that several factory workers getting off their shift at 11 o'clock one night last week saw angels who told them these things? And it was reported on the news. And reporters interviewed a dozen people who either saw the angels themselves or heard the account minutes afterward from people whose faces were lit up with shock and amazement all at once. What if you heard all that?

Would you pay attention? Would you be jarred out of the humdrum and sit up and take notice? Would you want to know more? Would you drive over there to the place it was all supposed to have happened and ask? Would you investigate? Would you look up prophecies in the Bible to see what it all might mean?

The birth of Christ is something amazing. It is worth thinking about, investigating with excitement and anticipation, because it is absolutely unprecedented and clearly miraculous.

Something Significant

Not only is Christmas something amazing: it is something truly significant. It's not just that it *is* something, but that it *means* something. Mount Saint Helens blowing up in 1980, or the Indonesian Tsunami in 2004 that killed nearly a quarter million people, are amazing events, but other than the self-evident warnings about seismic movements, they don't particularly mean anything. Not so with the virgin birth of Jesus. It is amazing, *and* it means everything. The truth it contains is colossal, revolutionary, astounding, and hopeful for the entire world for all history.

Perhaps you have not thought of Mary, the mother of Jesus, as a great thinker. But it's fascinating what was said of her in Luke 2:19. After the shepherds have come from the hillside nearby, seen the baby Jesus, and returned, after their report has been broadcast in the streets as they leave, after people have expressed amazement, and it's just Joseph and Mary and Jesus again in the place where the manger was, the Bible tells us Mary's reaction:

But Mary kept all these things, and pondered them in her heart (Luke 2:19).

Mary was not amazed, at this point. No doubt she was somewhat amazed when she first learned of her imminent conception from the Holy Spirit. You women and mothers, consider what you would have thought if you were told that you would shortly find yourself pregnant, that the baby would obviously not belong to any man, but that God himself would place a baby in your uterus, and that in nine months you would give birth to the Son of God. You would be amazed, at the very least.

Mary had probably gotten through the amazement stage. But then there was everything she had learned at first from Gabriel, and her discovery that aging Elizabeth would give birth to the prophet forerunner of the messiah, and what had happened with the sudden trip to Bethlehem in her last week of pregnancy, and now the strange visit by shepherds who told of being startled by angels on their hillside pasture. All this she had stored up, put in her mind, and *thought* about. She had meditated on it all, considered it, and no doubt sat and tried to figure it out.

Now the shepherds have left and she and Joseph and the cooing baby Jesus are left in the relative quiet of a stall, the deep dark around them, with perhaps a single lamp on top of the stall wall illuminating their little family. And Mary "ponders." She tries to take this latest piece of information, this latest evidence of the enormous thing God is "up to" in her very life. And though Mary knew considerably more than most people did about Israel's messiah at this point, it would be years before all

PONDERING CHRISTMAS

the pieces fit and she understood in detail what his role would be, and just *how* he would save his people from their sins.

Until then, she would "ponder," and think, and meditate, and keep on trying to understand. For that's what God's people do with what he shows them, and tells them, and does in their lives. They think, and they open their minds to God, and they ask him to show them more, and to help them understand.

Most of us are happy just to get through the Christmas season, have it all done and over, be done with all the big meals and spending and going here and there. We just look forward to doing nothing for a while. Can your Lord impose upon you for just a bit, however, to contemplate the significance of his birth, his coming to the world, his coming to you? Where would you be if he hadn't? Would you spend a little time in silence, thinking about what it all meant, what it all means, not only in time, but for eternity?

The Day After Christmas

'Tis the day after Christmas, the gifts are unwrapped,
The fir tree is shedding, my energy sapped.
We have to get out there and go to the mall,
To take back the sweater I got—it's too small.

The grey sky that yesterday looked like could snow,
Today is just dingy, and makes me feel low.
The websites report on the retailers' take,
And Christmas is judged by the money they make.

136

I'm far too inflated with turkey and ham,
And ready to call it off next year—I am.
This rushing, and buying, and eating must stop!
If I eat just one more iced cookie, I'll pop.

I want to have Christmas in silence one year,
To major on loving, and family, and cheer.
I want to help someone, to pass on the love
Of God, who sent Jesus, his gift from above.

I want to discover what Bethlehem meant—
The treasure of love in the baby God sent.
Next Christmas I'll feed on the word more than food,
And open my heart to the true Christmas mood.

I'll sing with new joy in my heart to the Lord,
For Jesus, his gift that I could not afford.
I'll make Christmas different, I'll do it, I vow,
O Father, why wait? I'll start doing it now.[27]
Robert Simms

The birth of Jesus Christ is something amazing. More than that, it's something significant, for the world, but also for you, individually.

- It means you don't have to make up for past sins; you can't anyway. God has sent a Savior to die for them.
- It means you don't have to live with fear of death or what lies

beyond. God has sent a Savior to give you the assurance of eternal life.

- It means you don't have to go through trouble and sorrow and stress all alone. God has sent his Son into the world, and his Son has sent his Spirit into believers, to be our divine companion.
- It means you don't have to waste your life on yourself, and come to the end of your days with nothing to show for it but indulgence and futile deeds. God has sent Jesus to be our Lord, the one we were created to live for in the first place.

Have you pondered Christmas? If you have, have you discovered these things yet? They are what Christmas is really all about.

11

The Agony of Christmas
(Luke 1:26–38)

Each year at Christmas people become enthusiastic about all the joyous and wonderful things they don't have time for during the rest of the year. They begin to speak glowingly of peace and love, out of that condition of the heart we have come to call, "the spirit of Christmas." And at least for Christians, each year they magnify the happiness and good will that seem to all of us to typify the celebration of that earth-shaking but quiet event: the birth of Jesus Christ.

But have you ever given much thought to the agony of Christmas? Not your agony, but the agony of those whose deeds and lives brought to us that Christmas event that now spells joy to all who celebrate it with understanding. To us, Christmas is happiness and cheer. To them, however, it most certainly involved some agonizing moments and situations.

Consider the suggestion that it was, and is, the agony of this Christmas event that made possible our present Christmas joy, but that without the full realization of the pain that attended the events in Bethlehem, there cannot be a full appreciation of the mirthful effects it has bequeathed to us since that time.

Consider further the urgency for us to make a personal acknowledgment of this agony, to the extent that we sense what was really transpiring in those months during which our Christmas story was unfolding.

Emotional Agony

There was certainly an emotional agony to Christmas. In several ways, the nativity of Jesus brought pain into specific human hearts and lives.

There was Mary's agony. Gabriel had appeared to Elizabeth with the totally joyous news of the coming birth of John, the forerunner of the Messiah. Nothing could have made her happier. But then, Gabriel appeared to Mary. What he told her had tremendous impact in terms of God's exciting work among his people. The Messiah was finally to be born. But Gabriel said to Mary, "You shall conceive, and bear a son." And Mary replied, "How can this be, for I have not known a man?"

Mary was a virgin and, though pledged to Joseph, she was unmarried. Consider what this meant to the girl. She was probably no more than fifteen or sixteen years old; she was betrothed, but not married; and she was pregnant.

It is easy for us to say, with our distance of both years and culture that such a predicament was not so bad. After all, she was with child by the Holy Spirit: no illicit union with another man was involved. She and Joseph had contained their desire for one another while they were only engaged. There was no shame in her condition; rather, there was one of great joy and awe. And, no doubt, she felt these things intensely.

Except. She couldn't escape the agony of it. She was pregnant out of wedlock. We don't know when she told Joseph. Matthew's account is unclear.

If she told him right away, the damage to her social life would have been minimized significantly. But if she did, did she explain everything? About Gabriel and the Holy Spirit and the baby's being the Son of God? It would be unlikely for her to tell Joseph she was pregnant without mentioning the encounter with Gabriel. If she had told Joseph all this, however, perhaps Luke would have said something about Joseph's not believing her at first, instead of merely implying it in describing Joseph's plan to quietly divorce her.

If, on the other hand, she didn't tell Joseph until he confronted her, wanting to know about her baby bump, then the social damage would have already been done. This seems less likely than that Mary told Joseph right away, because the word "quietly," which Luke used in describing Joseph's plans to divorce her, implies that he was trying to make the whole situation fly under the radar.

At any rate, Matthew's gospel says when an angel told Joseph in a dream what was going on, he moved Mary out of her parents' house and into his own, marrying her on the spot. That helped, but people can see and do the math, and they may have suspected presently that she and Joseph had jumped the gun a little bit.

While being unmarried and pregnant apparently means little to many women these days, there is no doubt that Mary was subjected to some cruel, malicious gossip. We don't know that she told anybody other than Joseph for a long time about Gabriel and so on. Eventually, somebody she did tell became the source of Matthew's gospel account. But even if she confided in someone early on, and it got around, her friends had seen no angel. Nobody else had ever become pregnant without sexual intercourse with a man. Doubtless nobody sat around having theoretical conversations about the possibility of parthenogenesis. Mary probably did not attempt to explain the facts of her condition to anyone except Elizabeth, and of course Joseph, who was, himself, straightened out on the matter by an angel.

If all this surmise is accurate, then as far as people were concerned, Mary had done something shameful, and no doubt they subjected her to scorn and ostracism. Some people may only have shaken their heads and thought to themselves how foolish this young girl had been.

Mary almost certainly felt this agony. Being accused falsely has a way of bringing as much internal misery as being accused justly. It wouldn't have been pleasant to lose friends and suffer stinging criticism and hurtful lies. It wouldn't have been easy to bear up under the burden of rejection by people who did not, and could not, understand. It was agony!

Joseph shared that agony. When he found out about Mary's pregnancy, he didn't know the details, but for a short while at least, he went through torturous hours of personal agony. He felt used, cheated, certainly betrayed. In his painful deliberations he finally decided to carry out a private cleavage of their betrothal, to try to spare Mary as much public embarrassment as possible, but also to escape the accusation of guilt he would most assuredly share if he remained with her. And then came the angelic announcement to him in a dream: "Fear not to take unto you Mary as your wife. For she is with child by the Holy Spirit."

If Joseph told everyone he was planning to divorce Mary (break off the betrothal—a more significant relationship in those days than engagement is now), then his acquaintances would have know why. When he subsequently married Mary, it would have been as a brave, forgiving, but cuckolded man, which would have carried an agony itself in the embarrassment. If he didn't tell anyone what he was planning to do, they would have assumed that he was the father of the child. Either way, he was likely in for some ridicule or disdain.

The angelic dream clarified in his own mind the truth of the matter. But it also locked him into a situation in which he would, as Mary, receive the emotionally wounding blows of public indignation and disapproval, to the extent that people figured out that Mary was pregnant before she and Joseph got married. No doubt, he withstood it gracefully. But being human, he could not have helped but experience agonizing hours inside himself, smarting from the rebuke of others.

When the months of Mary's full term neared their end, the couple were faced with an inconvenience that worked hardship on their already strained emotions and stamina. A degrading and humiliating sort of "world registration" was to be taken of all the Roman Empire. Caesar was counting his cattle, and his resentful subjects were required to go to the towns of their birth to be catalogued.

This meant that Mary and Joseph had to travel to Bethlehem, and she was in the ninth month and final days of her term. Over the rocky, bumpy trails they plodded, to please the whim of the Emperor. There was sheer, physical agony in that journey. But when they got to Bethlehem, there were no available spaces in the lodging houses. Apparently, Joseph had no relatives he knew in the City of David, or they were already crowded with other distant cousins and couldn't take two more, especially with another one on the way.

So, away from home, with no place to go, they holed up perhaps in a cattle stall, maybe in a cave-like stable on a hillside. And with no decent bedding, and possibly with cattle for companions, they tried to survive. And in such a state, Mary's labor began. Surely, their predicament was painful.

We paint with great beauty the stable scene, and imagine the sheep and oxen in some transfixed state of divinely imposed awe. We tell the story as if no one were aware of or cared about the difficult situation or the uncomfortable surroundings of that night. But we remember too easily what we were not in attendance to observe.

Likely all our imaginations of the idyllic scene in that stable, if it was a stable at all, are only fictional misrepresentations of what was experienced there the night Jesus came into the world. Surely, to Mary and Joseph there was a sense in which the arrival of their child was beautiful, and it transformed their surroundings into something special. But we should not doubt that they found themselves frustrated and inconvenienced by the particulars of their child's birth.

The emotional agony of the first Christmas was complex. But another kind of agony was ubiquitous in humanity, and painfully simple.

Physical Agony

Childbirth was almost certainly a typically agonizing experience for Mary. There does not fail to be a recognition in a woman that great joy comes out of this laborious suffering. And, in a real way, that expectancy diminishes the weight of the pain. But the agony of delivering a child remains.

But the agony of Christmas did not end there. The physical agony continued. Some time after Jesus' birth, perhaps as long as a year or two, Mary and Joseph were still in Bethlehem, having decided to settle there for a while. And one day they were greeted by foreigners, stargazers and holy men of a country to the east, who had somehow perceived that a great personage, a king, had been born. They had made known their discovery to Herod, whose jealousy and insecurity prompted him to conduct a manhunt for Jesus, to have him killed.

Here's where the physically oriented agony was re-booted. An angel told Joseph to take the family into Egypt for safety. So, here they were again, on the road, fleeing from a misguided monarch, knowing that there was no reason he should care about Jesus, no reason to fear for his position. Briefly homeless, Mary and Joseph lived the agonizing existence of fugitives.

How that agony must have doubled when the news reached them that because of them and their child, hundreds of little baby boys in and around Bethlehem had been brutally slain! How they must have cried in anguish for the pain others had undergone for their having had a child!

The emotional and physical agony were only the *human* agony of that first Christmas. We haven't yet looked at the deeper, more significant agony experienced by One who is higher and holier than Mary or Joseph. For the agony of Christmas is not only that of man, but also that of God, himself.

Divine Agony

This isn't a word usually applied to God—agony. But think deeply about the concept.

Think of another, similar word used of God's "emotions:" grief. God was *grieved* that he had made humanity (Gen 6:6), he *grieved* over Israel (Psa 78:40), and the Bible exhorts us not to *grieve* his Holy Spirit (Eph 4:30). The word "grief" is not used in a merely anthropomorphic way in these verses. It describes the emotion God reveals in his word that he "feels." And it's very similar to agony.

Did God agonize when he sent his Son into the world? He did, indeed. It was not his intention, in the beginning, that man should ever sin. But he did. And it was that entrance of sin into the world that made the entrance of a Savior into the world an eventual necessity.[28] Because of the things that were necessarily involved in that entrance, and in the eventualities of Jesus' life, there was certainly an element of agonizing on God's part.

God is, of course, a loving God, whose very nature is to sacrifice for the objects of his love. And so, the decision to send himself in the person of his Word, his Son, into the world by a miracle of incarnation was surrounded by the Spirit of total willingness. God *wanted* to come to us. We had left him, and could not return to him without a bridge, without a redeemer. So there was what would have to be called a divine joy in God's sending his Son.

But the coming of that redeemer was still with agony. For it was for the express purpose of dying that Jesus was born. And it was not an easy and natural death to which God sent his Son, but an ignominious and horrible death on the most cruel of death instruments ever devised. More than that, it was to be a death in which God himself, in the Son, would experience the filth and burden of the sin of all mankind placed upon him, as he became the divine sacrifice for man's iniquity.

All this God had in his mind as he descended to the womb of Mary. All this God knew, even as he sent his messengers to the shepherds' hillside saying, "Behold, I bring you good tidings of great joy which shall be to all people." Indeed, that message could be given only if someone first experienced the agony necessary, the agony inescapable, in determining to become the scapegoat for sinful man.

The agony of God paid for the angels' chorus on Bethlehem's hill. The agony of God at Christmas bought the spark of hope in humble hearts that night. God was saying, "I agonize, so you may rejoice!"

So, it was not as we are often quick to tell it, this Christmas event. Amid the scenes of glory was the presence of a reality laced with agonizing moments, agonizing predicaments, and an agonizing God.

Place this truth firmly into your mental and spiritual foundations for the celebration of Christmas. Without this realization, it's altogether too easy to think of Christmas as all sweetness and light, a time of joy that has no roots in sorrow, a message of happiness that has no history of pain. Without the realization that Christmas began with agony, it's too easy to slip into the folly of supposing that God descended one night out of the blue, and began telling us to just love one another, and be happy, and have good will toward each other. There is no agony in that, no risk, no accomplishment on God's part, and no sacrifice.

A Christmas that has no foundations in the agony of God, and the shared agony of man in bringing it about, is no Christmas at all. For Christmas is the beginning of the story of one who was born to save us by dying. And not only so, but it's vain, as well, to celebrate the joy of Christmas, to make merry, to have happy holidays, if in your life, in particular, there is not the personal foundation of agony.

To pretend to have joy of heart if there has never been brokenness of heart over sin is shallow. You must first share the agony of God over your sin, if the real message of Christmas is ever to break forth in you and give you the real song of heavenly joy. For all the pictures painted of him, in the manger or otherwise, you will never really see the Christ as the Savior, and receive him as such, until you find the agony of Christmas, until you become broken hearted over your sin, the sin that moved God to plan the nativity at Bethlehem.

Above all things, then, contemplate your stand before the Lord. Comprehend the deep agony that God experienced in order to bring you the angel's message of hope and promise: "She will give birth to a son, and you are to give him the name Jesus, because he will save his people from their sins."

12

Why Does Christmas Make Us Afraid?
(Luke 2:9–10)

Somewhere around the beginning of November every year we hear everyone from advertisers to entertainers to church leaders to television talking heads telling us that Christmas is coming soon. And in addition to the promotion of commerce, most of them talk about the spirit of the season, the spirit of love, joy, giving, peace, and goodwill.

Many songs tout the Christmas spirit. And most of us who celebrate Christmas find ourselves acquiring a cheery mood for the season, from *somewhere.* We believe in the positive effect, the blessing, of Christmas joy, and we willingly subject ourselves to the things that stimulate it, such as decorations, festive food, buying gifts for loved ones, donating to charities, and of course, lots and lots of Christmas music.

Some people look forward to Christmas all year and can't wait to start early, buying presents, making cookies, and getting out decorations. These are the people who send those early

Christmas cards, who are the first to have evergreens on their mailboxes, and who make the rest of us feel guilty when they boast on November 15 that they've gotten all their Christmas shopping done.

Other people love Christmas but the closer it gets to December each year the more nervous they get, because they are procrastinators. They don't start doing much of anything until the day after Thanksgiving. Then they rush around frenetically to get everything done that they themselves, and other people, expect them to do. But finally, they not only get the decorating and gift buying done, but they also get themselves into a modestly festive holiday spirit. They can't help it. Something about diving into the traditions that have grown up around Christmas engenders a mood of cheer.

But amid the joys of the Christmas season we have all been made aware in recent years that there are some anachronisms:

Just one of them involves the very people for whom, as we've been told all our lives, the Christmas message was supremely meant: the poorest of the poor. Due to the date of Christmas, in most places in the U.S. other than its southernmost climes cold weather brings on a crisis in sheltering the homeless. Many people do not look forward to Christmas because it accentuates their great need. Of course, some of the poorest of the poor will count Christmas a blessing because of the kindness of an individual or a charity inspired to give extra and do more for the needy. But Christmas, when viewed as the season of gifts and decorations and celebrations, is the province of those who have the substance to afford these things.

All this judges Christmas, however, in precisely the ways conscientious Christians have protested it must not be judged or celebrated: by its economic impact, its material prosperity, its freedom from want. And though we often do evaluate how wonderful a Christmas it has been by its perfect family setting, or our lack of sickness or problems, or, to put it bluntly, "the size of our haul," we realize in our wiser moments that this kind of measurement trivializes the event that lies at the core of the holiday. Viewed in any of these ways, Christmas cannot help but be a disappointment for many a person.

But just as out of place is an attitude many of us exhibit from time to time: fear. Ever hear anyone say she dreads Christmas? Most of us have heard it, some of us often. Usually the frightening things in mind are: the tight schedule; the glut of parties; the regrettable assurance of our overeating and the aftermath of feeling bloated; the tension of shopping; the trouble of finding gift ideas; the exhaustion of traveling back and forth; the inevitability of headaches, physical or otherwise; and unpleasant encounters with predictable relatives or other people. Fortunately, there are other valid ways of regarding Christmas, but most of us have been touched by this syndrome of fearing Christmas at some time.

There were incidents of fear at the first Christmas. One of them, in fact, is right there in the story we love so much to read during the season, Luke 2:9–10. Luke tells us about the shepherds out in the fields watching over their flocks by night, when an angel of the Lord appeared to them and the glory of the Lord shone around them. And then what does Luke say? **And they** were *sore* **afraid!** (emphasis and exclamation mark, ours).

There it is: "They were terrified!" (NIV, HCSB, *et al*). And if you back up to the first chapter of Luke you will find:

> Mary: equally undone by the announcement of her pregnancy with Jesus;
>
> Zechariah: "startled and gripped with fear," when met with the message of the birth of John, the forerunner of Jesus;
>
> Herod: whose reaction to the Magi's arrival was to be deeply "disturbed," an inward fear that gripped him so powerfully that he subsequently sought the murder of the Christ child and was willing to slaughter perhaps hundreds of infants to accomplish it.

In the cases of Zechariah and Mary and even the shepherds, we quickly realize that angels had burst in on the scene. Surely that was a terrifying sight at first, being out of the ordinary and clearly an appearance from the spiritual realm. In each case, the angels' very first words urged their listeners *not* to be afraid, and apparently the fears were allayed shortly. But something in each case convinces us that their apprehension did not entirely leave. And in each case, the experience of these biblical figures speaks to the issue of our own apprehension—our fear—engendered by the Christmas season or its message.

Fear of Unreadiness

First, some of us experience a fear of unreadiness.

As evidence, take the case of Zechariah. After he had calmed down, the message the angel spoke to him about the birth of John sank in, but he answered, "How can I be sure of this?" He was an old man, whose wife was also older than normal childbearing years. But more than that, he was an old man in whose life nothing earth shaking had happened so far, and here was the announcement of his participation in the divine pageantry of the Messiah's coming. He was to be the father of the forerunner, which would make him an important influence.

Zechariah's first reaction was to get some assurance of the *truthfulness* of the angelic announcement. As a purely private matter, he didn't want to get his personal hopes up for fatherhood if the angelic appearance was just a hallucination. But a more public concern was that he didn't want to go around reporting this significant event in the history of the nation if he was just to be ridiculed when it didn't come to pass. And anticipating that it was, indeed, going to come to pass, his question showed how apprehensive he was about the import of this development for him and his wife.

In other words, Zechariah was afraid. He feared the unknown ramifications of being an important part of a long awaited event and the focus of Israel's history.

Obviously, we twenty-first century people were not chosen to be a part of that event in history. We live long after it took place. Nevertheless, we Christians have a role in repeating both the message of John and the message of Jesus. And because we do, we are just as apt to be afraid of something that confronts us in the Christmas message. Because the message about Christ's

154

coming continues to contain this element of "making ready a people prepared for the Lord" (Luke 1:17), as the angel said to Zechariah about his future son, John.

This angelic word about "making ready" is a message about repentance and contrition. And we sense this, beneath the consciousness of celebration that we try to adopt the day after Thanksgiving. Essentially, the restatement of the message that makes us a little apprehensive is this: If Jesus is coming, and we are to be part of those preparing the way, will we qualify?

You might think this is taking the idea too far. People might claim that they are not at all afraid. In fact, if anything, they might be a bit bored with Christmas. But the fear of unworthiness and unreadiness prompted by the Christmas season shows up in simple and obvious ways. People even have a way of asking the two questions together when talking with small children: "Are you ready for Christmas? Have you been a good boy/girl?"

Adults still get asked the "ready" question, and we would say it means only "are the decorations all out, have you bought all your presents, and planned all your meals." But it may also imply, Have you turned on the Christmas spirit yet? The implication is, If not, why not? When Christmas day arrives, will you be happy and at peace? Is the message of Christmas joy just a phrase on a Christmas card, or is it what you genuinely feel?

By the way, people may not ask, "Are you a good boy," much anymore, not as much as in a previous generation, but don't we still worry about it? The temptation is to butter up our friends (and that goes doubly for the boss at work) in order to insure a nice present. And of course, we prove our worthiness if, in being given a present, we are careful to give one of equal value. How many of us would claim we were never afraid we would be embarrassed to have given a gift worth X dollars to someone who gave us a gift worth 5X dollars? That's why we *trade gifts,* as we sometimes say, or *exchange* them: we're afraid of being thought stingy or thoughtless.

The bottom line is that this Christmas spirit seems to be an attitude we believe we must *achieve* in order to be the kind of people who celebrate it—to deserve it, in other words. And we get apprehensive about developing that attitude, which consists largely of spiritual values like love and charitableness and kindness and being worshipful. And if, in these ways, we never do "get ready" for Christmas, we feel something has passed us by. If only we had been better prepared!

Our feeling of guilt for failing to achieve the Christmas spirit we think we ought to have is not much mitigated by reminding ourselves that God never told us we had to have a celebration of the birthday of Jesus. The fact is that we do have such a celebration. And even if we were tempted to forego it, we'd probably be afraid to do so because everybody else expects us to celebrate it. So some of us go on trying to find a Christmas spirit and having more trouble doing it every year.

This apprehension about Christmas is probably a very good indicator about the state of our spiritual lives in general. It's not surprising that we can't get emotionally and spiritually ready for Christmas if it has been essentially a year since we last engaged in similar spiritual exercises. After all, what is there about "the

Christmas spirit" that isn't descriptive of the way Christians should live *all year long?*

Unfortunately, many of us have a habit of falling into semi-consciousness spiritually, not really worshiping so much as dissecting preachers and choir performances. We tend to legalize our Bible reading, compartmentalize our discipleship, ration our service, and generally turn our spiritual lives into practiced ceremony. Undoing a year's worth of this behavior in a month already cluttered with purely secular emphases is apt to be increasingly difficult if not eventually impossible.

The remedy to this apprehension may take more than one Christmas to take effect. But it lies in realizing and internalizing a couple of things:

1. God sent his Son not because we were *worthy,* but because we were *unworthy,* and needed forgiveness and a new beginning.

2. Continued "readiness" for the approach of Christ to us does not rest on our *innate* worth, but our *imparted* worth: we are worth his love because God made us, and because he declares us righteous in Christ.

Zechariah represents the fear of unreadiness. There is also a fear of the unknown that crops up in the Christmas message. For that, we shall have to look, without some of the traditional reverence, at Mary.

Fear of the Unknown

The same angel who visited Zechariah went to Mary. She, too, was startled by the appearance, and Gabriel also said to her, "Do not be afraid." And, at least from the words written in Luke 1, the fear she felt at the first moment subsided. But Mary, too, questioned the angel, as Zechariah had done.

The really interesting thing about Mary's question, compared to and contrasted with that of Zechariah, was that Mary was not rebuked as he had been, or punished (in a sense) as he was for unbelief. Why?

The difference was in the question asked and the attitude behind it.

- Zechariah did not believe, and he asked for proof. "How can I be *sure* of this?"
- Mary believed, and asked for understanding. "How will this be, since I am a virgin?"

By the way, translations that say, "how *can* this be" improperly render the Greek verb, giving the impression that Mary was questioning the truth of Gabriel's announcement. She wasn't. She was perplexed as to the method of the fulfillment of the angel's words, but she wasn't doubtful of their truth. When her question was answered, she confirmed her initial belief with her submission: "I am the Lord's servant: May it be to me as you have said."

Where in the encounter of Mary with Gabriel is her fear of

the unknown?

- Mary's fear started in her being "greatly *troubled* at his words."
- Her fear continued in her heart-pondering of the strange visitors to Bethlehem and their report of angels.
- Mary's fear is reflected in her painful and apprehensive remembrance of Simeon's words. (Who else but Mary would have been the source of this incident?) Simeon said, "A *sword* will pierce your own soul too."
- Her fear is perhaps also glimpsed in her diligent remembrance of things (as in Luke 2:19, 51) where she "pondered all these things in her heart."

The Greek scholar A.T. Robertson suggested that there may be in these verses a hint of Mary's premonition that Jesus would soon be "beyond her mother's-reach." By the time Jesus was in ministry, this slight apprehension of Mary's came to flower, as she joined others in being very uncertain of her son's mental stability, urging him to come home, wondering if he was "beside himself."

It would be going too far to say that Mary was ever *overcome* by fear of the unknown, but it is clear that she was frequently a bit apprehensive about what her son was to be and to do, and what would happen to him.

This doesn't mean she responded to her apprehension in a wrong way. In fact, few people respond better then she did. And it's not wrong to find oneself feeling uncertain of the future. But not all of us respond so well.

Jesus' future is the gospel story we know: it's history to us now. But our own futures in his will lie ahead of us. What are they? What lies ahead for us if we walk the road with Christ? His disciples didn't know he was headed to the cross, not at first. There came points when they were tested about their resolve to go the distance with him.

As for us, we know Jesus went to the cross; however, some of us believe that our own trip to the cross will be largely symbolic and won't cost us much. But occasionally we're uncertain of this thought with which we have comforted ourselves.

We look at Jesus in the manger, shepherds in the field, glowing faces of many admirers, and we know it turned ugly on many fronts not far down the road. How long can our own idyllic Christian lives remain colored with the gentle pastels of Christmas card pageantry? How long will Christian life for us be just one pastoral setting after another before a Gethsemane and a Golgotha loom before us and test the mettle of our commitment and spiritual strength? In days of almost unthinkable revolution in America where the tide appears to be turning against Christian morals and religious liberty, how long will it be before Christians have to choose between the safety of silence and suffering for speaking up.

Non-Christians have some of these fears: 'If I become a Christian, how radically will God want to change my life? If I become a Christian, how much ridicule, loss, or persecution will come my way?'

Christian young people, in particular, are challenged to be

fully devoted to Christ and are invited to make seminal decisions expressed well by the hymn, "Wherever he leads, I'll go." They may fear that he might send them as missionaries or make them pay some high price for their devotion.

Many of us have had such worries. They may not be so much our fear of the troubles themselves as whether we would be spiritually mature enough to meet them. One of the wonders of God's way with us, though, is that we are often not mature enough for the trials headed our way, but when they happen, they bring us that maturity.

To risk quoting a pop song by the Rolling Stones, "You can't always get what you want / But if you try sometime, you just might find / You get what you need." On a deeper level than what the Stones probably meant, Christians who go through what they didn't want to, and who fear they won't be able to bear it, find that as they look to the Lord, they get what they need to endure and come out blessed, stronger, and closer to Christ.

What will it mean if you follow Christ? When you look down into that manger at Jesus, in your mind's eye you may sense that he has come for you. If you consent to follow him, what will he involve you in? What will he demand of you? Pastors everywhere have heard people express their fears of obeying the call of God in these very words.

The solution to this fear of the unknown is to confess, ironically with Mary herself, the character of God:

For he that is mighty hath done to me great things;

and holy is his name. And his mercy is on them that fear him from generation to generation—He hath filled the hungry with good things (Luke 1:49-50,53).

Everything that God plans for the followers of his only begotten Son may be described as "good." You may not know what it is, and at the moment it may look otherwise, but what *he* plans is something good.

After reading the story of the shepherds, it becomes evident that they show no lingering fears at all about the message of Christmas, even after the overwhelming, awe-inducing event with angels, more of them than had appeared to Mary and Zechariah. And remember, they hadn't been just startled, or even gripped with fear: they had been *terrified.* But after the angels said to them—angels must have said this a lot through the ages—"Do not be afraid," the shepherds did not show any further fear, at least as far as the written account goes.

They had a little conference and immediately decided to check out everything they had been told. And after finding everything as described, they went away ecstatic with praise and worship. Everything was wonderful!

How simple they were, how ready to believe and to respond in obedience! We don't know and can't reliably guess anything about their spiritual lives or preparation for this moment, but the evidence does show that they were humble, receptive and obedient.

What is there to be afraid of in Christmas? Well, this Jesus child may want us to give up any other plans we may already have had and follow him. He may want our lives to be as humbly lived as his was begun. He may lead us into the place of the cross, and ask us to die with him there.

But if we learn Jesus' lessons about discipleship: that they who lose their lives for Christ's sake and the gospel's will gain them; that they who humble themselves shall be exalted; and that if a grain of wheat falls to the ground and dies, it will produce many seeds: then what?

We should cast aside our fears, and go to see this thing which has happened, which the Lord has told us about. For God wants the simple faith of trusting hearts, and when we trust and obey there will be no reason to fear.

13

Born To Be King
(John 18:33–37)

Few themes echo in Christmas carols more than the kingship of Jesus.

- "The manger of Bethlehem cradles a king." ("There's a Song in the Air")
- "Born a child and yet a king." ("Come, Thou Long Expected Jesus")
- "Come and behold him born the king of angels." ("O Come, All Ye Faithful")
- "Glory to the newborn king." ("Hark, the Herald Angels Sing")

The carols say it because the Bible says it: "Where is he who is born the king of the Jews?" asked the Magi. The prophets confirmed it when they quoted Micah 5:2 to Herod: "Out of thee shall come a ruler over my people." Baby Jesus was born to be a king.

What did all this mean to those who understood it, whether they liked it or not? How did Jesus convey this truth to us, or did he? What should we make of it, that he is King Jesus?

The gospel of John, like the gospel of Mark, has no birth narrative. John's comment on Jesus' birth was encapsulated in language reminiscent of Genesis 1:1 and it presents to us the essence of the incarnation: "The Word became flesh" (John 1:14). But then, in John 18, the evangelist recorded the words of Jesus about the meaning of his birth. In the words he spoke to Pilate we have the answers to our questions about Jesus' kingship.

> Pilate then went back inside the palace, summoned Jesus and asked him, "Are you the king of the Jews?"
>
> "Is that your own idea," Jesus asked, "or did others talk to you about me?"
>
> "Am I a Jew?" Pilate replied. "It was your people and your chief priests who handed you over to me. What is it you have done?"
>
> Jesus said, "My kingdom is not of this world. If it were, my servants would fight to prevent my arrest by the Jews. But now my kingdom is from another place."
>
> "You are a king, then!" said Pilate.
>
> Jesus answered, "You are right in saying I am a king. In fact, for this reason I was born, and for this I came into the world, to testify to the truth.

Everyone on the side of truth listens to me."

"What is truth," Pilate asked. With this he went out again to the Jews and said, "I find no basis for a charge against him" (John 18:33–37 NIV).

This was one of the few commentaries Jesus ever gave on his own birth. It is important to know what he said about his coming into the world. Here, he tells us.

He said he came to be a king—testifying to the truth, and gathering subjects who will receive him as their sovereign. This entire conversation with Pilate, like many Jesus had with Pharisees, was about understanding the kingdom of God, recognizing Jesus as wearing the crown of that kingdom, and realizing what it meant to be a part of it.

Situated as we are 2,000 years later, our need is nevertheless the same. We are very worried on a day to day basis about the kingdoms of this world—we call them governments and countries.

- We fear kingdoms at war and perpetual conflict.
- We struggle against kingdoms that export terror.
- We complain about kingdoms that tax and spend.
- We worry about kingdoms that are crumbling.

Our concerns are not ill founded. But what we need most is to be aware of the kingdom of God, and be a part of it, through our relationship to its king. For every other kingdom is doomed to oblivion, but the kingdom of God is eternal.

Christmas is about the eventual overthrow of the world's kingdoms by the ruler of the universe himself, and we who want to be on his side *then* must come to his side *now.*

Jesus was born to be king. That claim is of interest not only to long-dead Israelites, but to very-much-alive Americans. The claim is relevant because Jesus is very much alive and present in the world today, and he's building his kingdom. Many people don't believe or understand that, but it's true.

Some people think that Christianity is an invention of Jesus' followers, not Jesus. A 2005 book by a professor at UT Austin is one of the latest "scholarly" works to promote this idea. Author Michael White goes so far as to say that what Christians made out of Jesus was something Jesus himself never conceived of.[29]

Some people think the idea that Jesus fulfilled Old Testament prophecies is just his disciples' reading back into the Bible what they wanted to believe. But this scripture in John, where Jesus tells Pilate why he was born, is like many others that show that Jesus knew he was born to be king.

Hebrews 13:8 says that Jesus Christ is the same yesterday, today and forever. What he was doing then, he is still doing today. The kingdom he started is still growing, and will soon displace every earthly kingdom. Those who understand that fact, and who receive Christ as King in their own lives, will prosper. Those who refuse his sovereignty will ultimately be punished.

Jesus Knew Who He Was

We need to see two things in the passage from John 18, and

to believe them without question. First, Jesus knew who he was.

There are few more destructive things being taught, even in some Christian colleges, than the idea that Jesus didn't know who he was, that his disciples later did all of the necessary Old Testament interpretation to identify him as the Savior and King, that they proclaimed what Jesus had never said, himself. Many a religion student has had to study books such as Gunther Bornkamm's *Jesus of Nazareth,* which said that Jesus didn't think of himself as the Messiah, certainly not as the Son of God. Many a course in Christianity has been taught by a professor who agreed with this viewpoint.

The only way you can say such things is to tear out vast portions of the Bible, especially the gospels. Not only do you have to eliminate whole books, but you also have to expurgate verses here and verses there within books such as the gospels, on the assumption that you know better what they should contain than the early church fathers who preserved the writings and declared them to be divinely inspired.

You have to assume that the Holy Spirit's inspiration of the Bible was mostly suggestion and that the writers were given license to fabricate and stretch the truth—to lie, in other words.

When you've done all this editing of the Bible, on the presumption that you know so much, then you can say that Jesus didn't know who he was. But if you take the Bible the way it is written, without arbitrarily deleting Jesus' reported words, and if you take the Bible with the utmost respect as most Christians do, there's no way to reach that conclusion. Jesus, in fact, did know who he was.

- He said, "Before Abraham was, I am" (John 8:58). He knew he was the pre-existent Word of God.
- He said, "I and the Father are one" (John 10:30). And even as early as the age of twelve he told his mother, "I must be about my Father's business" (Luke 2:49). He knew he was the Son of God.
- He said, "The Son of Man came to seek and save those who are lost" (Luke 19:10). He knew he was the incarnate deity.
- He said, "For this hour I am come" (John 12:27). He knew he was the Savior.
- He said, "For this cause I came into the world" (John 18:37). He knew he was the King of Heaven, to earth come down.

Since the Bible gives us truth, we know that Jesus knew who he was. And who he *was*, is who he *is*. He is the King of Heaven, the eternal Word of God made flesh.

Jesus knew not only who he was, but why he was here.

Jesus Knew Why He Was Here

As he stood before Pilate, he capped off the witness he had given so many times before about his purpose. He said, "For this reason I was born, and for this I came into the world, to testify to the truth."

We should notice three things about what Jesus said. First, Jesus told Pilate that he, Jesus, was born to be king. Pilate had grilled Jesus about whether or not he was a king. The Procurator seemed to rest his disposition of Jesus on the matter of his right to a throne. If Jesus were an heir to some throne, trying to generate rebellion against Rome, Pilate would have to deal with him; he would have no choice but to do so. Jesus said that he was born a king. We know from Jesus' lineage that he was an heir to the throne of David. He could have claimed it, though he didn't.

Second, Jesus told Pilate not only that he was born a king, but also that he came *into* the world, meaning that he came from somewhere else—he existed before he was born a human being. This simply reinforces everything else Jesus had said about himself. In one of his parables, he spoke of himself as the son sent by a landowner to his tenants. In that parable, the son was killed by the tenants, which is what Pilate was about to order at the insistence of the Jews. In the presence of his disciples, Jesus prayed, asking the Father to glorify him with the glory he had with him before the world began. In other words, Jesus was saying he was before us and came from beyond us.

Third, Jesus told Pilate the purpose of his coming, the essence of his kingship: to testify to the truth. He is a king; he is the King of kings. But he had not come at that time to claim the political throne of David in rebellion against Rome. He posed no threat to the jurisdiction of Pilate as governor. His kingship was over a different kind of kingdom, a kingdom of truth. That's what he explained briefly to Pilate.

Pilate didn't understand what Jesus was talking about. He thought he had posed the unanswerable question when he asked Jesus rhetorically, "What *is* truth," and then left the room. But it's clear enough what Jesus was talking about. Truth is everything that God says. It is everything that is right and good. It is what

God says about himself, about creation, man, his purpose, his sin, and his need. It is whatever God has revealed, and it is personified in Jesus himself, who said, "I am the way, the truth, and the life." If you want to know what truth is, look at Jesus.

Jesus' kingdom isn't connected with any land, doesn't exact any taxes, doesn't wield political power, doesn't have an army, doesn't threaten any ruler anywhere, at least in the sense that most heads of state would be concerned about. This kingdom transcends geography, governments, politics, even history itself. Jesus' kingdom was, and is, the collective lives and resources of those who believe in him and follow him as the source and embodiment of truth. His rule in their lives makes them citizens of his kingdom.

A woman known to be nearly deaf came to church faithfully every service, sat in worship, and appeared to be taking in every word. Somebody asked her one day, "Why do you keep coming? You know you can't hear anything that's being said." She said, "I know, but I keep coming because I want everybody to know what side I'm on."

Siding with the truth is the essence of citizenship in God's kingdom. Jesus is the king who proclaims that truth, and siding with Jesus is what being a Christian is all about.

When Jesus was born, he was referred to as king by the Magi, who troubled all Jerusalem along with Herod by their visit and their inquiry about a newborn regent. Herod became frantic with rage and fear because of his assumption that a newborn king posed a threat to him and his lineage. Herod became the spiritual father of all who would try to kill the kingdom of God by persecution.

If Pilate, on the other hand, had any sense at all what Jesus was saying, he dismissed it as unimportant. He assumed Jesus' kingdom was a figment of his imagination. He became the spiritual father of those who would try to kill the kingdom of God by indifference.

But neither persecution nor indifference will stop the progress of God's kingdom. Jesus was born to be king, and Jesus lives. And all who receive him as king receive his life. They begin living eternal life when they receive him, and nothing can take it away.

Jesus said of his kingdom, "The kingdom of God does not come with your careful observation, nor will people say, 'Here it is,' or 'There it is,' because the kingdom of God is within you." And to Pilate Jesus said, "My kingdom is not of this world." And Paul wrote of this kingdom, "Flesh and blood cannot inherit the kingdom of God." And this fact is why *the crucifixion of the king didn't kill the kingdom.* It just delivered the king back to the throne room of heaven, from which he now reigns.

A few years ago there were grand ceremonies and festivities in Washington as the last stone in the National Cathedral was laid. The building was begun in 1919, having been suggested by President George Washington more than a hundred years before that. It took eighty years to complete. The Cathedral is actually an Episcopal church building, but most people think of it as belonging to the country. It is supposed to stand as a symbol of the ongoing religious life and conviction of a country which still prints on its coins, "In God We Trust."

In a small way, the National Cathedral illustrates how the kingdom of God spans time, generations, and political administrations. The kingdom of God itself, of course, spans all human history, crosses every political border, thrives on every continent, and survives every plague, persecution, cultural revolution or war. It survives and thrives because it is *not* a worldly kingdom.

But simply because it is not a kingdom of this world doesn't mean it isn't real. It is far more real than any other, because its King is eternal, because its subjects are permanent, and because it will outlast every government and nation on this earth. In fact, all their political power and geographical claim will finally be turned over to Jesus, as this present age comes to an end. The book of Revelation depicts the angel of the Lord at the coming of Christ saying, "The kingdoms of this world are become the kingdoms of our Lord, and of his Christ, and he shall reign forever and ever" (Rev. 11:15).

It seems so idyllic, so quaint, so "nice" to sing Christmas carols, and so seldom does our excitement rise above the serenity of the nativity scene, even when we sing words like, "The manger of Bethlehem cradles a King," or "Glory to the newborn King." Perhaps we ought to think it through again. Here was the King of heaven, come to call us into the eternal kingdom of God, demanding of us a choice between allegiance to this world and utter allegiance to him. To sing at his manger suggests we are ready to surrender to his throne. Is it true of you?

14

Dreams of Christmas
(Matthew 1:18–2:25)

The observant reader who pores over chapters one and two in Matthew will be struck by the dreams that played a part in the revelation of Jesus' birth, and then the guidance of Joseph and Mary through that time of turmoil and danger when Jesus was born. One of the first questions the thoughtful reader must ask is why so many dreams were required. Was it:

(A) The normal channels of spiritual leadership were not working well?
(B) There was great interference from spiritual adversaries? or
(C) God was simply adding supernatural drama to a spectacular, though temporarily obscured event?

Perhaps it was (D) a bit of all of the above. And the more one reads the account, the more it seems that Matthew was aware of the recurring pattern of dreams, and that he himself thought that pattern to be significant. In his narrative, he didn't provide any explicit commentary on the dreams, but perhaps between the lines there is implicit meaning. Like biblical archeologists, we should dig a little to see if we can unearth that meaning.

The dreams took place over a span of twenty-six verses in Matthew 1 and 2.

> ...the angel of the Lord appeared unto him in a dream, saying, Joseph, thou son of David, fear not to take unto thee Mary thy wife...(Mat 1:20).
> And being warned of God in a dream that they should not return to Herod...(Mat 2:12).
> ...the angel of the Lord appeareth to Joseph in a dream (Mat 2:13).
> ...when Herod was dead, behold, an angel of the Lord appeareth in a dream to Joseph in Egypt...(Mat 2:19).
> ...notwithstanding, being warned of God in a dream, he turned aside into the parts of Galilee (Mat 2:22).

Speaking only from what we know, God used five dreams to direct the course of events involved in the nativity of Jesus. Joseph was the recipient of four of those dreams, and he was the indirect beneficiary of the remaining one. It appears that all along the way during the time of Jesus' birth, God was orchestrating events in such a way as to make certain that all went as he had planned.

Other than showing us the paramount importance of Jesus' safety as a vulnerable child, these dreams also have a contemporary word for our own living. They tell us that as God works out his plans, he reveals whatever is necessary for us to be able to believe and obey him. Sometimes—well, to be honest, with many of us it's *most* of the time—we have difficulty arriving at just what God wants of us. Or, our best senses are not sufficient to position us where he wants us to be. We may occasionally fail to discern God's directions, but God never fails to give us the leading necessary to involve us in his purposes.

Let's focus first on that idea, that God involves us in his purposes. This is really the perspective we need:

God's Priority: His Own Purpose

Often the most important thing to us is what the will of God *for us* is. That's the way we usually pray: O God, show me your will. The unnecessarily redundant triad of petitions we often hear from church members called on to pray is, "Lead, guide, and direct." We seem insistent that God show us what he wants us doing. In all this urgency to find out what *our* purpose is, we may pay too little attention to what *God's* purpose is.

The distinction may seem fine, but don't miss it: the most important thing is not what the will of God *for you* is, but what God's own purpose is, irrespective of *your* role. It's not your part, or mine that matters, but God's purpose, whether or not we participate.

God is never defeated

It's vital to make the distinction between the *intrinsic* will of God and the will of God *for you* because it's crucial to understand that no one defeats God. His purpose cannot finally be frustrated. Even when someone resists the will of God, the unconquerable Lord has already, from eternity, woven that resistance or disobedience into his universal plan.

We testify to our belief in God's thorough victory when we pray the words Jesus suggested to us: "Thine is the kingdom, the power and the glory" (Mat 6:13).

- It's no one else's kingdom: though Satan has tried to build his own kingdom and subvert God's, he is shortly to be shown what an awful failure he has been, despite what appears to be evidence to the contrary.
- It's no one else's power, either: all powers on earth and in the spiritual realm operate under the inscrutable permission of the Almighty, and those who operate against him are simply being given enough rope to hang themselves with.
- And finally, it's no one else's glory: in the end, every knee will bow and every tongue confess that Jesus Christ is Lord, to the glory of God the Father (Phi 2:11). No pockets of the counterfeit glory of pretenders will remain anywhere in the universe.

This overarching principle that no one defeats God is reflected in the description of the dreams of Christmas, the messages given to direct Joseph and the Magi.

The focus of the dreams

In contemplating these dreams you may be inclined at first to focus on Joseph, their recipient. Because the initial dream was meant to straighten out his thinking about Mary, you may begin to see the other dreams as guiding *him,* and as benefitting *him.*

For instance, the first dream saved his upcoming marriage. The second dream, to the Magi apparently, bought time for Joseph in Bethlehem. The third dream helped Joseph care for the safety of his family. The fourth dream freed Joseph to return home, and the fifth dream fine-tuned his decision on a place to live.

But what were these dreams really about? The comfort of Joseph? The safety of Joseph? The fulfillment of Joseph as a person? Not primarily. Joseph's comfort, safety and fulfilment were wonderful byproducts, but they weren't the central reason he was given the dreams. The primary reason was to protect the infant incarnation of God's Eternal Word, little Jesus.

Look at the dreams again.

The first dream took place when Jesus was yet unborn. Joseph was prepared to divorce Mary because he presumed she had slept with another man. In the dream, God told Joseph to go on with the wedding, because the child was not of human origin. The principal beneficiary here was Jesus, not Joseph. God wanted Jesus to have a whole family, not to be born illegitimate and/or be raised without a human father. It was essential to his upbringing and to other details of God's plan.

The second dream was to the Magi, we presume (the most

natural reading). But this dream told the "wise men" to circumvent Jerusalem on their way back home. Again, it was Jesus who benefitted. He would surely have been killed by a crack team of professionals if the Magi had gullibly gone back and blabbered everything to the devious Herod, who had no intention of going to worship Jesus, but rather to eliminate him.

The third dream was like the second, another chess move by the Almighty to protect the King of kings who as yet could not protect himself. (By the way, think of that astounding irony!) The angel who appeared in the dream told Joseph to move to Egypt for a while. Joseph might have been endangered if he didn't, and certainly the death of his son would have devastated him. But it was Jesus who was being protected.

The fourth dream sent Joseph back home, but again, it wasn't for Joseph. Yes, he had probably left a profitable carpentry business in Israel and he likely needed to return to it in order to make a decent living for himself and his family. But it was principally for Jesus that the family returned. It was for his upbringing in the culture of his homeland and for his future ministry, that he was returned to Israel.

The fifth dream specifically placed Jesus in Nazareth, the most immediate reason being his protection from the realistic, lingering possibility of assassination by Archelaus. The son, Archelaus, knew his father Herod had tried to wipe out all the babies in Bethlehem just to eliminate the one he was afraid of, but that's the last the royal family knew of the possible whereabouts of the baby born to be "king of the Jews." We plausibly assume that no one knew his family had moved to

Egypt, and when they came back, they could not be traced easily to Nazareth. It is as if you were being sought by authorities in Chicago, you escaped to Mexico, and then you came back much later and very secretly to Enid, Oklahoma. These days, of course, you would have to do all sorts of other things to hide your identity. But you get the point. God was protecting his Son.

In every case, it was Jesus, not Joseph, who was the chief focus of Joseph's dreams. God's purpose was bringing Jesus, his only incarnation, from infancy to manhood and to the cross, to conquer sin and death.

Don't misunderstand: Joseph was not unimportant to God. After all, God involved Joseph in his plan in a notable and blessed way. But it was the plan of God *itself* that was most important to God, and Joseph knew that.

The 1989 film *Field of Dreams* was a wonderful depiction of the role of baseball in American life, among other things. In the film, Ray Kinsella, played by Kevin Costner, is a young farmer whose father, now dead, was a baseball player a couple of decades before. The two were estranged from Ray's teenage years.

One day, Ray hears whispering in his field of corn: "If you build it, he will come." He follows the directions he hears. He builds a baseball field out in the middle of his Iowa farm. The voice turns out to be from Shoeless Joe Jackson.

Kinsella travels around the country urging several other people to come to Iowa, including a disillusioned writer, Terrence Mann. But meanwhile, the ghosts of dead ballplayers come out of the corn every day and play on the field.

At a high point in the story, the players are finished for the day and have gone to the outfield and disappeared into the corn. Shoeless Joe stands some distance away and looks toward the group: Ray, his wife, and Terrence Mann.

Joe says, "Hey, do you want to come with us? (back out into the corn)."

Ray says, "You mean it?"

But Joe says he means Terrence Mann, not him.

Ray loses his cool for just about the first time in the story, and he says: "Wait a second. Why him? I built this field. You wouldn't be here if it weren't for me. …I want to know what's out there."

Joe says Ray isn't invited, but Ray says, "What do you mean, 'not invited'? That's my corn out there. You guys are guests in my corn. I've done everything I've been asked to do. I didn't understand it; I haven't once asked what's in it for me."

Shoeless Joe says, "What are you saying?"

And Ray falters a bit and then says, "I'm saying, What's in it for me."

If you saw the film you know that shortly, after Terrence Mann disappears laughing into the corn, Ray Kinsella looks toward the mound and sees a new player, one who hasn't been on the field yet. When the player turns toward the sidelines, Ray realizes it's his father. The film ends with a touching reunion between the two, as they play catch, on a field of dreams for them both.

The point of the scene is that Ray had his eyes on seeing what was in the corn, when Joe had a much higher purpose in mind for him.

Now, this wasn't a religious film, and the higher purpose Shoeless Joe had in mind was the reunion of a father and son. But the story illustrates how we can get caught up in what we interpret as the plan of God *for us,* and narrow the scope of our spiritual vision to that, so that we begin to make decisions, to consider the options for our course of life, on the basis of our envisioning what *we think* we're supposed to be or to do in God's plan. And while that doesn't sound altogether wrong, if that's how we approach things, we may well be leaving out what God's plan *overall* is. Because his overall plan, his intrinsic plan, may not include giving us long life, putting us in a place of public acclaim, providing us with a peaceful existence, etc.

Read the early chapters of Acts sometime and stop when you get to Acts 12:2. Shortly after the beginning of the church, Herod arrested James, one of the apostles, and had him summarily executed by the sword. James. One of the twelve. Newly anointed with the Holy Spirit. Present at Pentecost. One of the evangelists who led thousands of people to Christ as the Holy Spirit moved. One of the leaders of the nascent church. Going places. Honored by all.

Dead. Why? His brother John made it to his late eighties at least before he died—in exile, yes, but after a long career in the church. Peter, shortly arrested by Herod, who had the same purpose in mind for him, was delivered by an angel and went on to live a fairly long life, building the church among the Jews as Paul did among the Gentiles. Early church documents other than the Bible tell us that several other apostles went here and there and lived on for years, spreading the gospel. Andrew and Matthias to the north, perhaps as far as what is now Russia. Thomas and Bartholomew to the east, maybe as far as India. Philip to the south to Africa. Matthew to Persia. They went to the four points of the globe.

But James was eliminated near the start of things. Why?

Only God knows why, ultimately, but that's kind of the point, isn't it? What was happening in James's life was not about James so much as it was about God's overarching purpose. We in turn must come to see ourselves subsumed in the larger purpose of God.

And by the way, did you ever consider the likely fact that by the time Jesus began his ministry, his father Joseph was no longer in the picture? Most theologians believe he died previously. He wasn't around to see what became of his son, not from the visual perspective of earth, anyway. No doubt he was kept abreast of things in the bosom of Abraham, but for all that dreaming and hearing angelic warnings and directions, for all that traveling and protecting and providing, he left this earth before the plan of God came to fruition in the life and ministry of his son, Jesus.

This little tidbit also illustrates that what matters is not whether *Joseph* got to see the outcome or participate in it somehow, but whether God's ongoing, eternal plan was fulfilled. It's *always* about God's intrinsic plan, not ours, or even about our place *in* God's plan. Keep the focus on God's plan, God's kingdom, God's power, and God's glory.

Especially in these modern times of self-centeredness, it's easy for us to fall into preoccupation with ourselves, our fulfillment, our prosperity, our wellness, our wholeness, and on and on. It's often pointed out that the overwhelmingly best-selling books are what we might call "self-realization" materials. For many people, the universe revolves around themselves. If this attitude is brought to a quest for God's will, it can seem to us that our own place in God's will is the most important question for us. In reality, what is most important is God's own plan, period. We should exalt his plan above any part we may or may not play in it. And our only personal concern should be faithful obedience to any detail we're asked to perform.

Consider Moses. If he had finally refused to go tell ole' Pharaoh to let my people go, would that have canceled God's plans? Hardly. God would have gotten another Moses to play the part of Moses.

If Jonah had decided, three days into his encounter with fish gastroenterology, to decline the call to Nineveh, would God have given up on the Ninevites? Almost certainly not. He would have found another prophet, and Jonah would have been digested.

God *involved* Moses in his plan to free Israel. God *involved* Jonah in his plan to save Nineveh. God *involved* Joseph in his plan to redeem all mankind. But they were not the stars of the show. God's plan was the main show, and Jesus was and had always been, the main character.

All this is not to say that we should ever disparage the will of God for our lives, as if it didn't matter to God whether we did his will or not. If it didn't, he wouldn't call us to do it. Once we have firmly fixed in our hearts and minds that it is the success of

God's plan that is vital, not our own success as measured by any lesser standard, then we may indeed be earnest about finding and doing his will for us.

God does, in fact, involve us in his eternal plans. To do so, he has to get the message across to us. To accomplish this, he uses various means. Essentially, God's procedure is to customize revelation.

God's Procedure: Custom Revelation

Joseph had at least four dreams that gave him information along the way, information that ultimately protected Jesus. The nativity stories are filled with unusual supernatural events. Zechariah had a vision in the temple. Mary had a visit from an angel. Shepherds suddenly had company drop in while they were tending sheep. The Magi discovered a major astronomical sign.

Did you ever notice that everybody else got waking visitations, while Joseph had dreams. Why?

We aren't in any position to say with finality why, but whatever other reason there was, certainly we may say that God deemed it the best way to communicate to Joseph what he wanted to say. It was tailored to the recipient.

Tailored revelation

We have a hint of the reason for dreams just before the first one was given. Joseph found out that Mary was expecting. We know he must have been broken-hearted. Everything we know about Joseph tells us he was respectable, godly, and righteous.

His response to the crisis was measured. He weighed the fact that under normal circumstances he shouldn't consider continuing with wedding plans given Mary's state, presumed to be the result of pre-marital unfaithfulness to him. Over against that, though, showing his remarkable compassion, he gave loving consideration to Mary's own reputation, and he decided on a very private cancellation of their engagement. Given the facts as he knew them, and given his character, he was making a wise, and ordinarily a very godly decision.

This was the problem: ordinary godliness was not sufficient in this case. He didn't know that Mary's baby was not even Mary's (much less another man's), but was the Word of God incarnate. Today we would say that she was the surrogate mother of the Son of God. Even if Mary had tried to tell him, which she may not have done, there was no precedent for this kind of thing, no compelling reason for him to accept at face value the claim that her pregnancy was supernatural. Put yourself in his shoes. If he were to act any differently than he planned to act, he would have to have a special word from God. That's where the tailored revelation came into play.

When God had to get a special word to Noah, he spoke audibly. When God called Moses, he lit up a bush. When God sent Isaiah, he burned his lips clean. When God converted Paul, he struck him blind. God decided to speak to Mary's Joseph in a dream about the incarnation of Christ.

The point is, God used the method necessary to communicate his message. He customized his communication to the needs and circumstances of his target, in this case, Joseph.

Have you ever had somebody tell you about how God "spoke" to them? Sometimes people can be terribly obnoxious about their encounters with God. Some folks apparently believe that their experience is normative for everybody else. In other words, if you haven't heard from God as they did, you haven't heard from God. Just for an example, if God had spoken to some of these religious television personalities as often and as audibly (or visibly!) as they say he did, we should have seen some pretty dramatic things out of them by now. That we haven't is sufficient commentary on the legitimacy of most of them.

But the fact is that God doesn't speak to all of us in the same way, or even to any one of us in the same way every time. He doesn't cater to us, but he does customize his approach. He tailors his revelation to what we need, to be able to hear and understand it.

God's bottom line in revelation is to communicate. That's why the Bible is not an obscure book, despite some people's suggestion that it is meant to be dark and mysterious. It isn't. God means for his word to be understood. Sometimes he reveals himself in such a way as to stymie the efforts of the haphazard, casual or unbelieving reader to understand it. But the studious, devoted, believing reader will always be permitted to discern truth.

That principle applies to worship as well. What communicates to one person may fall flat on another. The various trends in "worship style" have been referred to as "worship language." Some people's worship language is ultra modern, some contemporary, some traditional. Some speak "cowboy church." Some understand best the language of ancient symbols.

For the most part, we can't change the language of worship we understand. The things God uses to move you to conviction, confession, or commitment may not speak to me, and vice versa. What we have to do is not to copy somebody else's experience, but instead seek God for ourselves, preparing our hearts for his word by humility and submission. When God speaks, he will choose the best way to be heard.

It would be unkind, of course, to suggest that all "real" Christians will have supernatural visions or messages from God. For many of us, most if not all our guidance will come from the internal witness of the Spirit, making the words of the Scripture personal and compelling. That's why it's so important to be acquainted with the great promises of God, and to learn to detect in our regular reading of the Bible the message God has for us today.

And when God promises something, he always keeps his word.

God's Promises: Always Kept

Consider what happened as a result of all these dreams of Christmas. Every one of them served to direct the people involved so that God's promises and the prophecies of his prophets were fulfilled.

Step by step

Keeping his prophetic promises means that God directs the lives of his servants, his people, and even the course of history and its secular and unholy movers and shakers, so as to fulfill his plan step by step.

The first dream kept Joseph from making Mary a single mother and Jesus a fatherless child. Matthew writes that Joseph received this dream so that the prophecy of Isaiah would be fulfilled: "Behold, the virgin shall conceive and bear a son, and *they* shall call his name Immanuel." Notice the word "they." It may refer to the two parents, who would be the ones to name the child. While Joseph and Mary didn't give Jesus the legal name "Immanuel," which means "God with us," they did name him "Jesus," which means "The God who saves," or "God Saves." Saving us is what God came to do when he came to be "with us."

But even more significantly, "Immanuel" is not as much a personal name of Jesus of Nazareth as it is a name he would come to be known by for the work that he would eventually do.

The second dream, which came to the Magi, protected Jesus and it changed the plans of Herod. Instead of killing one baby, he killed many. It was a sad, prophetic word that was fulfilled, but it was part of what God foreknew would have to take place.

The third dream took Joseph and family to Egypt, again in fulfillment of prophecy, that the Son and Messiah would be called out of Egypt. This prophetic reference goes back to the exodus of Israel from bondage, which, as many Old Testament events, was a **type** of future things, a sort of historical foreshadowing of similar but more significant events to take place later.

The fourth and fifth dreams belong together, guiding Joseph back into Nazareth as Jesus' boyhood hometown. Under the impress of the Holy Spirit, Matthew saw the prediction of the Messiah's being called a Nazarene as a reference to Nazareth, rather than to his being a Nazirite, which may or may not relate to the name of the town. (We looked at the term in chapter 8.)

To many people, some of these things might seem like minor details, but no detail of Jesus' life was insignificant.

God's attention to detail

Certainly God was not haphazard in planning the birth, upbringing, or influences on the life of the Savior. But just in case you assume otherwise about your own life, realize that no detail of our own lives is small to God, either. He cares about everything in our lives. It goes without saying that he hasn't prophesied in Scripture the course of every person's life, but don't you think he knows every one of them? This is the meaning of the term "omniscient," which we apply to God.

In fact, David says in Psalm 139:16, "All the days ordained for me were written in *your book* before one of them came to be." The Bible is too small for all of our individual lives to be detailed, but God's book, the mind of God, is unabridged. He has worked out every detail in his ideal plan for you, as well as every contingency plan that will ever be needed, and he cares about everything you do. While the overall plan of God is supreme, his plan for you is comprehensive, even if, as is always the case, you don't know much about it. It unfolds step by step.

This planning means that God is prepared to lead you every step of the way, including taking charge after missteps and failures, rebellion and prodigal living. When you ask God for guidance, he will give it. James says if we know we lack wisdom (which means we're humble about it) and ask God with faith (which means we trust God with our lives) that God will lead us by his wisdom without scolding us.

And among the things that will verify for us the genuine leading of God is this invariable fact that God's leading will always be consistent with his written word, the Bible. He doesn't violate his own principles. Just as every dream led to the fulfillment of prophecy for Joseph, Mary and Jesus, every impartation of guidance to you will help you fulfill what God has already had written in the Bible for your general direction. One of the best ways to test what you think God is leading you to do is to compare your notion with the written word of God. If there is conflict, your notion is not of God.

If you had been Joseph, would you have understood what these dreams you were having were accomplishing? Would you have realized that God was working out a grand purpose much larger than your life, and that he was inviting you to be involved? Would you have believed what he revealed to you, and would you have trusted and obeyed completely? Would you have seen how God was fulfilling his plans through your own life and that of your family? Would you have praised God for his grace in including you? Would you have committed your life to the service of God all your days?

God's great purpose is to give you eternal life through a change of heart, bringing you back into his family. He has given you this message in the nativity histories and in every gospel message you have ever heard, about Jesus the Son of God who came to die for sin and rise for victory over death. And God has confirmed the truth of his word to you in a thousand ways through the Scriptures, and in the still small voice that tells you in your inner heart that his way is true and every other way is a dead end.

The dreams of Christmas are not about fiction, fantasy, or embellished children's stories. They are truth from God to people like you and me, news of a very real Savior, who waits to enter your life, or having entered it, to fill and control it completely.

15

Christmas is Not an Island
(Matthew 2:10–12)

In the Indian Ocean lies a little dot of land called Christmas Island. It was named on Christmas Day in 1643 by English Capt. William Mynors. What a nice, idyllic name!

Christmas Island is now an external territory of Australia. It's typical of many ocean islands. Condé Nast Traveler describes it as "a lush, off-the-beaten-path tourist destination famed for its caves and coral reefs. The biggest yearly attraction is the migration of fifty million red crabs down to the sea to spawn."[30] It's kind of like a lot of small, ocean islands: a retreat from the rest of the world.

The author has never had the yen for an island vacation. The attraction of these islands is mostly the artificially exotic things some resort developer has built. The island itself may not be much different from the one Chuck Noland—Tom Hanks's character in the film *Cast Away*—was stranded on for four years. The author imagines a week on a resort island would seem like that long. But apparently most everybody else thinks going to an exotic island would be the ideal getaway.

Australia's Christmas Island doesn't have evergreen trees, snow, or crisp winter air. But *our* Christmas island does. You know, the one we visit each year when December comes and we take a time-out for the biggest American celebration of all. Christmas has become an island for us in many ways.

- It is a retreat, or at least we imagine it is. Something about getting in the Christmas spirit serves as a remedy to the attitudes we have been harboring all year long. We're ready for a break.
- It is a change in routine. Most people's daily lives change around the Christmas season. Some businesses do more business at Christmas than during the other eleven months combined. Some do less.
- It's a time of personal changes. There are more shopping trips, outings, hustle and bustle, parties, and much, much more eating. Our checkbooks and wallets take a hit.
- It's an excursion into beauty and refreshment. Though most of us have complained about the rushing around and the plethora of things to be done at Christmas, one appeal it has is getting away from the usual scenery and humdrum pace of life. We decorate our houses and yards as if they were someplace enchanting and magic, we get into a mood of gaiety and good will, and we refresh our spirits.

While there isn't anything inherently wrong in Christmas's

being a much needed retreat, an island of a different time in the sea of our day-in, day-out lives, there is something to question about it: is that what Christmas is *meant* to be?

Or can we say what Christmas is meant to be? Elsewhere, we've noted that the Bible contains nothing requiring us to hold a celebration of Christ's birth, so there can't be any authoritative rules once we've decided to have a holiday. The way each of us observes Christmas is up to us.

But if the Christmas story and its implications are to be important to us, there are some things that look like purposes in the celebration of the nativity. They are the lessons that come out of the scripture passages that tell us of Jesus' coming to the earth as a baby.

One of those passages universally regarded as being about the nativity is in Matthew 2, the story of the visit of the Magi. This account isn't really about the birth of Jesus. It's about the visit of eastern astrologers to the home of Joseph and Mary somewhere around the time Jesus turned two. We know this from scriptural evidence among other things. But the facts haven't kept believers from having the Magi show up at the same time as the Bethlehem shepherds, all of them crowding the manger scene. It didn't happen that way.

There's no vital point to be made from this inaccuracy of tradition, but there are some very important points to be made from the visit of the Magi itself. These lessons speak to the appropriateness of our observance of the nativity of Christ. The key verses for our inspection are 10-12:

When they saw the star, they were overjoyed. On coming to the house, they saw the child with his mother Mary, and they bowed down and worshiped him. Then they opened their treasures and presented him with gifts of gold, frankincense and myrrh. And having been warned in a dream not to go back to Herod, they returned to their country by another route (Matthew 2:10–12 NIV).

Perhaps there aren't any scriptural rules for Christmas, but surely there are some things that serve the purpose of celebrating the birth of Christ and some that don't. If Christmas isn't to be an island of artificial irrelevance, an island of mere escapism, an island of meaningless frivolity, then what should it be?

The unwritten rules in fact *are* written, in the illustrative stories of such people as these Wise Men. In their example, as unlikely as these astrologers are to constitute one, we find ways to keep Christmas from being an island. Surely Christmas should be first:

An Opportunity to Find New Love for Jesus

Perhaps we can't really call what the Magi felt "love," but Matthew says they were overjoyed to have found the place where Jesus was and that when they came into the house, they *worshiped* him. That sounds like adoration. Dozens of classical as well as modern paintings of the visit of the Wise Men are officially titled "The Adoration of the Magi." The concept is inspired by the scripture itself.

Certainly God wants far more from us than mere expressions of devotion; he wants lives that are obedient. But in at least one sense, love for God is much like love for anyone: it needs expression to stay warm and keep growing.

Of course, it's easy to say, "I love you," and not really mean it or live it. But the person who is tender and deliberate about the expression of love is likely to grow in the reality of that love. To say, "I love you," helps you to feel it. To feel it helps you to act on it. To act on it is to make it real. For love is an activity more than a feeling.

All of us need to love God more. Most of us need to tell God of our love more than we do. Specifically, most of us need to express our love and affection for Jesus Christ, the Word of God come down to us, more than we do. Nowadays we aren't gazing into a manger and seeing a baby, but hopefully we are gazing heavenward into the face of the risen Christ, who went all the way from the cradle to the cross for the purpose of saving us.

It's hard to countenance that Christ and not love him. It is hard to take in the ultimate purpose of that sweet nativity and not be moved to some deeply rooted, appreciative love as a matter of response. Christmas should certainly be a time for finding new love for Jesus.

We commonly call the Magi the Wise Men.[31] They were probably from Persia and were likely Zoroastrian astrologers, part of a priesthood dating back to the time of Daniel and before. There were three of them, or twelve of them, or any number of them, depending on which non-canonical traditions you look at. The prevailing tradition in the western world is three because there were three specified gifts, but we don't know.

We also don't know anything about their knowledge of Jewish scriptures though they obviously had some. We don't know if they had any secret affiliation with Judaism; probably not. Because they assumed the king of Judea would know about the birth of the next king, it's likely they didn't have any inkling that the king they concluded had been born was a king of an entirely different sort. The bottom line is that in their coming to Judea with their lavish gifts and a caravan of who knows how many people, we don't know how much their "adoration" qualifies as a genuine expression of love.

But Matthew's purpose for including the story about the Magi was to give us an example of an expression of honor and adoration by the peoples of the earth, befitting the King of kings come from heaven. If we don't get out of that story a lesson about intensifying and growing in our love and worship of Christ, then we aren't paying attention to the scriptures.

Most of our softer Christmas carols give the impression of looking down into a manger with quiet awe and love. For the Magi, there was no manger, but we can easily picture in our minds their gazing at a mesmerizingly perfect two-year-old boy and realizing that he was to be a king of unsuspected, unsurpassed greatness. Our mental depiction of the adoration of Jesus' early visitors is one reason the music of some carols is so hauntingly lovely. And we tend to have feelings of warmth and affection when we sing them.

We usually don't fail to find some revival of love for our Savior when Christmas comes around. Surely that's one thing Christmas is for, and it's one way to make sure we aren't just cruising to Christmas island when December 25 rolls around.

As long as we're going to celebrate it, another thing Christmas should be is:

A Way of Reinstating a Pattern of Giving

Ultimately, our tradition of giving gifts traces to the Magi's offering of gold, frankincense and myrrh. To this day, jewelry stores and perfume counters see a lot of Christmas buying every year.

There are many ways we could critique the nature of our gift giving habits. If we're honest, we would have to mention our regrettable use of the phrases, "trading gifts" and "exchanging gifts." We would be obligated to reflect on the extravagance of our giving to one another when compared with our gifts to the Lord through his church. But on the plus side, consider simply the benefit of our having a special day for establishing and reestablishing the principle of giving in our lives.

We should let this lesson from scripture not just reaffirm our traditions but also shape them. We shouldn't be content to give to just that inner circle of family and friends. If Christmas is to cause us to reflect the fundamental elements of that nativity in Bethlehem, we must allow the giving spirit to take on new dimensions in compassion and charity. Somehow, we ought to give something of ourselves or our plenty to someone not normally in our little world. Preferably, someone new ought to be taken into our world and included in our love just as God reached out and included us in his.

Before retirement, the author was included yearly in a Christmas Eve breakfast hosted by a major law firm. The central feature of the breakfast was the promotion of the firm's annual charity, which changed every year. Over the years it became evident there was plenty of need and there were many, many worthy causes. Those who ate breakfast were challenged to write a generous check to the annual charity. It was a great way to encourage people to touch more and more lives with their substance.

The specifics of growth in giving will differ in every life. This book can't say how creative giving should manifest itself in the reader's life. In fact, the inspiration to give in new ways may change every year. But the principle is clearly there, first in the gift of God, and also in the example of the Magi. Look how far they traveled to bring gifts to Christ. Doesn't it suggest to us that a good guideline for our expansion of the spirit of giving is to go out of our way? It wasn't a convenient gift the Magi gave. Their journey was the very definition of inconvenience. How should their example speak to our own giving?

Finally, the Christian's thoughtful generosity should not be simply an imitation of someone else's. By design, it should be personal. In fact, when we blithely imitate others, it's often by way of finding a minimalist example, thereby justifying our own paltry offerings.

Everybody else may be sailing to the Christmas island of trendy symbolism. When we think about our giving and we give out of a consciousness of what God has given us in Christ, we cannot limit ourselves to symbols. We find we are compelled to give substantially and with a spiritual focus. Christian faith inspires a spirit of giving that is distinctively different. Random giving doesn't fill the bill. Generic generosity isn't enough. For the Christian, Christmas should also be:

A Time for Renewing Our Missionary Purpose

Christmas is an ideal time for mission emphases in the church, not only because the general emphasis on giving lends itself naturally to mission offerings from the congregation, but first and foremost because Christmas is a missionary story.

Christmas is God's missionary excursion into planet earth to bring salvation to the people God made. Shouldn't we find in Christmas year after year a time to engage in missions ourselves, as the carriers of the message of redemption? How inconsistent with the coming of Christ if the church of our Lord Jesus Christ doesn't find itself moved into more devoted, fervent telling of the gospel as a consequence!

This Christmas blessing of the gift of Christ is not just for our little families, our little worlds, our little congregations, or even for the very large kingdom of *believers*. If, as the angel said, the good news "shall be to all people," then Christmas is not to be a private moment of reflection only. It begs to burst forth explosively into the world where it is needed.

Christmas is not an island! It isn't a time for us to go into holy, evergreen, candle-lit seclusion and revel only in the joys of our private good fortune, enjoying the longtime and comfortable love of our nuclear family. It isn't a time for us to indulge selfishness on an island of private enjoyment, to the exclusion of the world back on the continent of daily life.

Instead, Christmas is a time for reaching out, for recommitting ourselves to the goal of becoming people like Christ, who left his home in heaven to take us into his family. It is a time to find new affection for Christ the Lord, out of which we will serve him more devotedly in days to come.

NOTES

1. "Christmas Is," by Percy Faith, 1991.

2. "Christmas Is," by Francesca Battistelli.

3. Compare Heb 12:22 with Rev 5:11 and other passages and note translations that use "millions" to render the Greek of the latter passage.

4. The King James Version of the Bible is employed frequently throughout this book. The word "men" appearing in that translation often means "human beings." Sometimes, this book will use that two word term, sometimes not. In the parlance of the Bible, "man" is a term for humanity, male and female. We find no problem in using the term to refer to both men and women.

5. Georgia Knick Horne, "The Greatest Gift," ("The Gospel Hour," Greenville, SC, 1968) 25.

6. John H. Sanford

7. The term "X-mas" or "Xmas" is widely perceived in modern times to have been invented by anti-Christians in order to take Christ out of Christmas. In fact, an early variant of it was devised in 1551 by Christians. It has a long use in Christian contexts. The Greek letter "X" *(Chi)* is the first letter in *Christos,* and was early used as an abbreviation for Christ's name. However, because of the fact that the English (and multinational) letter "X" ("ex") is a mathematical symbol for the unknown, the term "Xmas" has lately been assumed to be a circumlocution for saying the name "Christ." And, as in the world of politics, where "perception is reality," so here: If people use "Xmas" to avoid printing the name of Christ, it is exactly that, despite its actual history.

8. "One Solitary Life," by James Allen Francis, July 11, 1926, in a sermon delivered to a Baptist Young People's Union in Los Angeles, CA.

9. The Greek word commonly translated "inn" may also mean "guest room," and the newer editions of the NIV and some other versions render it so. If Luke meant the idea of a "guest room," possibly in a relative's home, then our entire concept of the roadhouse—to say nothing of an innkeeper—may be false.

10. Broadman Bible Commentary Luke-John. Clifton J. Allen, ed. Luke: Malcolm O. Tolbert. Nashville: Broadman Press. 1970) 29.

11. J. Norval Geldenhuys, *Commentary on the Gospel of Luke, New international Commentary on the New Testament*, (Wm. B. Eerdmans Publishing, Grand Rapids, MI, 1951) 101.

12. Elliott, Emily Elizabeth Steele, "Thou Didst Leave Thy Throne" 1864, in the public domain.

13. "We Need A Little Christmas," by Jerry Herman, in the Broadway Musical "Mame" (1966).

14. At a church the author once attended, a woman sang a song in which the lyrics wished Jesus a happy birthday When she was finished, the pastor of the church said there was nothing more appropriate for the hour than to wish Christ a happy birthday. The author objects strenuously and finds such sappy sentimentalism totally inappropriate for worship or any other context. The church and the persons involved are mercifully unnamed in this book, and this story has been confined to an endnote to avoid distracting the reader.

15. See the author's book, "Where Did I Come From" (published by Robert Simms and available at *lulu.com),* for a discussion of how the necessity of the virgin birth flows necessarily from a biblical understanding of how God created man and how man procreates body, soul and spirit.

16. "There Was No Room in Bethlehem," words © 1960 Hope Publishing Company, 380 S Main Pl, Carol Stream, IL.

17. This oft-printed quote has been attributed to any number of subsequent writers, many of whom who used it without citing the source: Herb Caen (1988), Thomas Friedman (2005), Christopher McDougal (2009) who attributed it to Roger Bannister, *et al.*

18. Stewart Simms, in "The Beams," the newsletter of the Beech Haven Baptist Church, Athens, Ga, Dec. 1986.

19. Don McCollough, Waking from the American Dream (?)

20. From "Good Christian Men, Rejoice," translated by John Mason Neale from a 14ᵗʰ century Latin text.

21. "Mary Had the Little Lamb," by Marv and Marbeth Rosenthal. Permission is granted by the authors to reprint without written permission from the authors.

22. "The Little Man Who Wasn't There," Lyrics by Harold Adamson.

23. "The Little Blue Man," Lyrics by Betty Johnson.

24. The story appeared in *The Reader's Digest* in 1966. It was told in a version other than the one above, which the author recalls from a later version of *RD* but cannot find. It was recounted by Ron Hutchcraft (*https://www.hutchcraft.com*) on Dec. 24, 2007 as having taken place in Cornwall (England? Canada?), and the punch line was different: there was no rivalry. Notwithstanding Hutcraft's insistence to the contrary, *snopes.com* labels the story as legend.

25. "The Innkeeper," attributed to a B. P. Baker, was published in autoillustrator.com (now defunct). We can find no further information about the poem's author. Most books and sites reprinting it say "Author Unknown."

26. From "Living for Jesus," by Thomas O. Chisholm, 1917.

27. "The Day After Christmas," by Robert F. Simms, ©1980. All rights reserved.

28. God's omniscience, of course, demands that we understand that God was not surprised by man's sin and did not have to "come up with" a plan of salvation. The timeless God is in all places, and in all times, all the time. This is the force of Peter's statement that Christ was ordained as the Lamb "before the foundation of the world." Paul made a similar statement about the choice of an elect people in Eph 1:4. The phrase is a linguistic stab at the concept of God's timeless decisions. There was never a time when he had not determined everything he would do *in* time.

29. L. Michael White wrote *From Jesus to Christianity* (HarperOne, 2005).

30. Ken Jennings, "Why There's More Than Once Place Called 'Christmas Island,'" (Condé Nast Traveler, *https://www.cntraveler.com/story/why-theres-more-than-one-place-called-christmas-island*, the Internet).

31. The term Magi or Wise Men (KJV *et al*) translates the Greek *magoi* (μαγοι).

www.ingramcontent.com/pod-product-compliance
Lightning Source LLC
Chambersburg PA
CBHW031254090426
42742CB00007B/455